PAULA NADELSTERN

PUZZLE QUILTS

SIMPLE BLOCKS

COMPLEX FABRICS

C&T PUBLISHING

Text © 2005 Paula Nadelstern
Artwork © 2005 C&T Publishing, Inc.
Publisher: *Amy Marson*
Editorial Director: *Gailen Runge*
Acquisitions Editor: *Jan Grigsby*
Editor: *Candie Frankel*
Technical Editors: *Carolyn Aune, Susan Nelson*
Copyeditor/Proofreader: *Wordfirm, Inc.*
Cover Designer: *Kristen Yenche*
Book Designer: *Rose Sheifer*
Design Director: *Rose Sheifer*
Illustrator: *Tim Manibusan*
Production Assistants: *Kiera Lofgreen, Tim Manibusan*
Photography: *Diane Pedersen* and *Luke Mulks*, unless otherwise noted
Published by C&T Publishing, Inc., P.O. Box 1456, Lafayette, CA 94549
Front cover: Detail of Block 1B
Back cover: Block 1C, Block 1F

Library of Congress Cataloging-in-Publication Data

Nadelstern, Paula.
  Puzzle quilts : simple blocks, complex fabrics / Paula Nadelstern.
    p. cm.
  Includes index.
  ISBN 1-57120-336-2 (paper trade)
  1. Patchwork—Patterns. 2. Appliqué—Patterns. 3. Patchwork quilts. I.
Title.

TT835.N334 2005
746.46'041—dc22

2005015583

Printed in China
10 9 8 7 6 5 4

Table of Contents

Dedication

To bright and
beautiful Ariel,
my new quilting
buddy

Acknowledgments

So many thank-yous, so little opportunity to convey them. That's why I'm going to grab this occasion with both hands and shout out my appreciation to the following people:

My editor, Candie Frankel. I knew you'd rush down the New York State Thruway to rescue a good read as soon as you heard my distress signal.

Amy Marson, Todd Hensley, Jan Grigsby, John Pilcher, and the rest of the C&T team, who try to let their authors write the books they have to write. Special thanks to Carolyn Aune for fine-tuning the manuscript technically, an aptitude I completely lack; I was beyond grateful to have a calm, skilled person to rely on. Same goes for Kristen Yenche, who worked very hard to uncover the quilt book cover that existed in my mind's eye, and Rose Sheifer, who tweaked an ordinary book package into a stylish book design. Thanks also to Lynn Koolish for understanding the importance of a few good latkes.

Photographer Bard Martin, for exposing a likeness I like.

Megan Downer and Katia Hoffman, who get my design sensibility and use their combined expertise to turn it into gorgeous goods. Thanks also to the rest of the Benartex team—David Lochner, Susan Neill, Alex Rodriguez, Esther Zelinsky, Lisa Hamm, Susan Kemler, Karlos DaSalla, Elizabeth Ahlering, Bill Mason, Gayle Camargo, and Yuduth Holguin-Tejada—for ensuring that my fabrics live as long a life as possible and for humoring me and my endless requests.

Phillip de Leon (Alexander Henry); Gail Kessler and Clifford Quibell (Andover Fabrics); Donna Wilder, Meredith Voltaggio, and Debi Porreca (FreeSpirit); Sandy Muckenthaler (Hoffman Fabrics); Jason Yenter (In the Beginning Fabrics); Evie Ashworth (Robert Kaufman Fabrics); Pru Bolus (Langa Lapu); Cathy Miller (Michael Miller Fabrics); Wendy Richardson (Quilt Tapestry Studio); Yuichiro Kyomori (Watanabe Manufacturing Company); Cosette Russell (Cosette Marbled Silks); and Joyce A. Robertson (Westminster Fabrics), for trusting me with their collections.

Martin Favre and Gayle Hillert (Bernina USA); Pat Yamin (Come Quilt With Me); H.D. Wilbanks and Darlene Christopherson (Hobbs Bonded Fabrics); Marti Michell (Michell Marketing); Peggy Schaefer (Omnigrid, a division of Prym/Dritz); Ted Finkelstein (Gutermann of America, Inc.); Clover (for my favorite yellow scissors); Quilter's Rule; and Rowenta Irons, for generously providing me with excellent products.

Deb Tilley, Linda Joy, and Shelley Knapp, for putting up with my shenanigans while they work very, very hard in my Quilt Festival booth. Thanks to Michael Miron, Shirley Levine, Stevii Graves, Debby Schwartzman, and Cindy Friedman for pitching in and to Wendy Richardson for shouting encouragement across the aisle. Also, a debt of gratitude to Deb for generously lending me her admirable talents and skills whenever I ask and to Lorraine Torrence who, to borrow from Tom Cruise, always helps me help *me*.

Cheryl Little and the knowledgeable, good-hearted gang of the Cotton Club, for supporting and encouraging my endeavors, not to mention inviting me to Boise every few years so this New Yorker can do some serious shopping. I'd also like to recognize the generosity of the resourceful staff of Tennessee Quilts for helping me turn an over-whelming situation into a great opportunity.

The late Margit Echols, who in 1983 made the first contemporary puzzle quilt, entitled *Patchwork Sampler Quilt*. Margit's contribution to the dynamic tradition of quilt design is gratefully acknowledged.

Katherine Knauer, for letting me use her clever phrase so everyone will think I am clever like her, and Robin Schwalb, who inspires me always and doesn't mind when I need to kvetch or need a TV program taped. As delighted as I am that Jeanne Butler and my dear cousin, Amy Orr, join us for Quilting by the Bay, mostly I am grateful that none of you accomplished artists are very fussy.

The members of The Manhattan Quilters Guild: Ludmila Aristova, Teresa Barkley, Jeanne Butler, Randy Frost, Iris Gowen, Tatiana Ivina, Emiko Toda Loeb, Ruth Marchese, Jeri Riggs, Diana Robinson, Robin Schwalb, Sandra Sider, Arle Sklar-Weinstein, Daphne Taylor, Ludmila Uspenskaya, Erin Wilson, and Adrienne Yorinks, for my monthly dose of creative juicing. I would be very thirsty without it. We will always miss our founding member, Karen Berkenfeld, a quiltmaker and friend of unequaled quiet grace.

Clara Lyman, my very supportive mother and summer housemate, who will run any errand in walking distance.

Eva Nadelstern, my mother-in-law, who helped put my studio back together when this task did not seem humanly possible.

Eric Nadelstern, who I hope will keep me laughing as hard through the next 35 years as he has through the last.

Spirals twirl through space. The vibrant colors of this four-fabric palette merge together, forging the illusion that there are no seams at all. Puzzle Block 2C (Workbook, page 60).

The soul of this book can best be described by a clever phrase bequeathed to the Manhattan Quilters Guild: *semper tedium*. Essentially, it means when there is a hard way to do something, we'll find it. And that's exactly what I plan to do here: teach you how to take a simple bunch of patchwork shapes that could be pieced together quickly and easily and, instead, make the process as precious and complex as rocket science. I not only want to seduce you into loving beautiful, complex fabric as much as I do, I also want you to see the stuff the way I do.

We all know that a good block design organizes an abundance of color and form into a coherent and pleasing image. But what does a great design do? Using the framework of a Puzzle Quilt, I'll try to answer this crucial question. In a Puzzle Quilt, the same block design becomes whimsical or elegant, a blockbuster or just a bust, depending on how various fabrics are used. It's the perfect medium for exploring how printed fabric can be used to vary one and the same patchwork configuration. If you are ready to embrace the potential offered by a wide range of fabric choices, to figure out what characteristics catapult a good quilt block of unassuming squares and triangles beyond the ordinary, then stick around.

> *"We all know that a good block design organizes an abundance of color and form into a coherent and pleasing image. But what does a great design do?"*

A Puzzle Quilt is a sampler quilt with a secret: each block design is used twice. By using totally different fabric combinations, the quilter creates the illusion that each block is unique. The "puzzle" is to pick out which blocks are the same. *Luminosity Puzzle Quilt,* 2004, 50" x 66", designed and machine pieced by Paula Nadelstern, machine quilted by Gayle M. Camargo. See the quilt diagram with block placement on page 50.

We'll start with elements of design and Paula-*isms*—theories that explain my idio-syncratic patchwork sensibility. Next, on to fabric and a set of attitudes I've cultivated, a way of defining and thinking about the attributes that fabric brings to the design table. To make two blocks with the same underlying structure look like they've landed from alternate universes, we have to be able to identify and manipulate these elements at will. To do that, we need to own them by understanding the role they play in design.

After looking at fabric from every angle, I'll show you a couple of clever template and piecing tricks I rely on to compensate for the fact that I don't really sew very well. (It's sad but true. I can go forward and backward on a sewing machine and I can make a knot, but that's about it.) Once you grasp my piecing rationale, visit The Puzzle Block Workbook (pages 51–89) and see it all come together in six different blocks, each one pieced in six different fabric combinations.

Keep in mind that my approach is to offer guidelines, not step-by-step methods; I'm describing a process, not giving you projects to make. I'm well aware of the fact—and you should be, too—that I made up most of this stuff. It's really neither right nor wrong, but since this is my book, I get to tell you my side of the patchwork story. When it comes to fabric—where color meets cloth—I'm a strong proponent of a "more is more" approach. Add to this conviction an optimistic respect for serendipity imparted by much experience. Now, instead of panicking when pushed into a piecing predicament, I know enough to recognize a happy accident and share control. You'll see: You, too, can become an agile user of uncommon fabrics, creating artful responses that are both deliberate and opportune.

Depending on your point of view, my liberal theory of abundance may be good news or bad. Realize, I might get overwhelmed when faced with a computer-generated learning curve or having to remember everyone's name, but when I land in a fabric store the length of a New York City block that's filled with industrial shelving packed with goods, I want to know why there isn't more.

Elements of Design

"You must decide the route you'd like the eye to take when it travels around the block."

A *quilter has as much right* as any other artist to think of herself as a designer. But if you want to walk the walk, you have to arm yourself not only with attitude but also with knowledge, specifically the classic elements and principles of design. Since this information is easily available in books and on the Internet, I'm going to highlight only the aspects most relevant for our purposes and include some of my own rudimentary assumptions. For homework, list the elements and principles of design in alphabetical order and use each one in a sentence.

Think of yourself as a tour guide, directing visual traffic. You must decide the route you'd like the eye to take when it travels around the block. Once you've made that decision, it's up to you to figure out which fabrics have the moxie to act like a trail of bread crumbs, leading the way. The elements you'll use are line, rhythm, symmetry, and color. With these four elements in your cerebral sewing center, you'll have a built-in navigation system that will enable you to control alignment, show direction, or mark a point of pivot.

Line

Art defines *line* as a moving dot, because the viewer's eye must move to follow it. Line turns out to be an expressive tool because each basic direction in which the dot can move—horizontally, vertically, or diagonally—has its own personality.

An intrinsic relationship exists between line and patchwork, since most patchwork blocks are divided into straight sewing lines. Depending on the choice of fabric, the seamlines can be camouflaged or accentuated. You can create lines in a block by highlighting the patchwork seams or by using lines already printed on fabric. Identical motifs are perfect for creating implied lines because the eye tends to connect similar elements automatically.

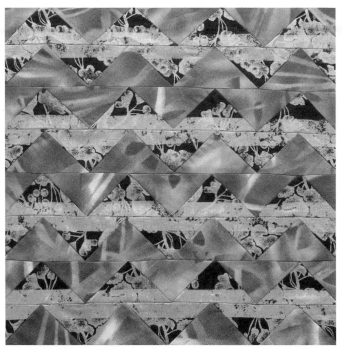

Horizontal lines move the eye across the block. A horizontal design imparts calmness and stability, calling to mind both the horizon and our sleeping posture.

Vertical lines are visually active. In this block, they suggest plant life that grows from the ground up.

Diagonal lines, slanting from corner to corner or radiating from the center of the block, imply imminent change. Movement in multiple and opposing directions creates the most dynamic effect.

Rhythm

Visual rhythm is based on repetition and refers to the movement of the viewer's eye. Identical repeating motifs cause the eye to leap from element to repeated element. Depending on the fabrics used, the pace and flow of this movement can range from a smooth, graceful undulation to a peppy, punchy march. There is a corresponding emotional response in the viewer.

Symmetry

Trust symmetry. We ourselves are symmetrical creatures, and symmetry is innately comfortable and comforting to our species. We welcome its balanced harmony.

Most traditional block designs are symmetrical. There's an inferred line down the middle of the block, with corresponding patches to the left and right. Choosing the same fabric for these mirror image pairs guarantees visual coherence. To up the symmetry quotient, you can fit intricate, symmetrical motifs cut from printed fabric into each pair of mirror image patches. When symmetrical motifs meet their mirror images, they reflect into something brand new and often unexpectedly beautiful. Symmetrical designs provide an elegant solution to many design questions, turning mundane into magic.

That said, I don't want you to think that symmetry is always the answer. It's just that I want you to permanently add it to your internal list of design possibilities.

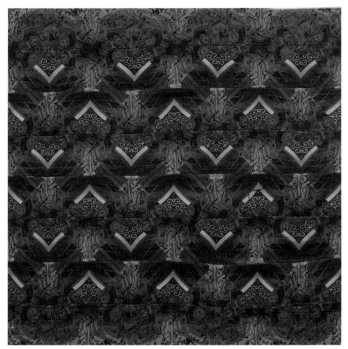

Gold V-shaped motifs flit across this dark block. The large number of motifs, and the fact that they face in two different directions, creates a rapid, staccato rhythm.

Agile patterns from a butterfly print fabric touch one another in multiple mirror image pairs, blossoming into a brand-new design with graceful continuity. See the original fabric on page 66.

Acts of Color

Color, for our purposes, is about fabric. An effective use of color has just as much to do with the relationships between colors as it does with the actual hues. It's all about using the colors in our fabrics to make some parts of the design stand out and other parts recede. Once you understand the innate characteristics of color, you gain control of the whole shebang.

Two key concepts that you should master are value and contrast. *Value* is the artistic term for light and dark. Value creates a sense of depth, the perception that some shapes are closer than others. In general, light values appear to advance while dark ones recede. *Contrast* is the relationship between these areas of light and dark. Areas of sharp contrast are dramatic and draw the eye to them. Areas of lesser contrast recede, suggesting distance. When the value contrast is minimal, the effect is calm and subtle.

The visual impression of depth is also affected by the color itself. The warmer colors—yellow through red-violet on the color wheel—catch the eye and tend to advance.

Relative color values organize the design into areas of sharp and mild contrast. Together, they define a block's visual unity.

Block 6E (rainbow, page 86) is shown right side up and upside down. Cool or dark tones create a weighted, comfortable stance, pulling the eye irresistibly downward as if by a force like gravity.

The cooler colors—yellow-green through blue-violet—tend to recede. But this is just a general guideline. The warmth or coolness of a color is always relative to the colors surrounding it. Some colors are more susceptible to mutation than others. Pure vibrant colors are less vulnerable to neighboring influences, while muted colors readily modify their appearance. That's why olives, mustards, and weird greens, the ones suggestive of a discolored bruise and affectionately referred to in the quilt world as "baby poop," turn out to be such versatile foils.

Weird Greens

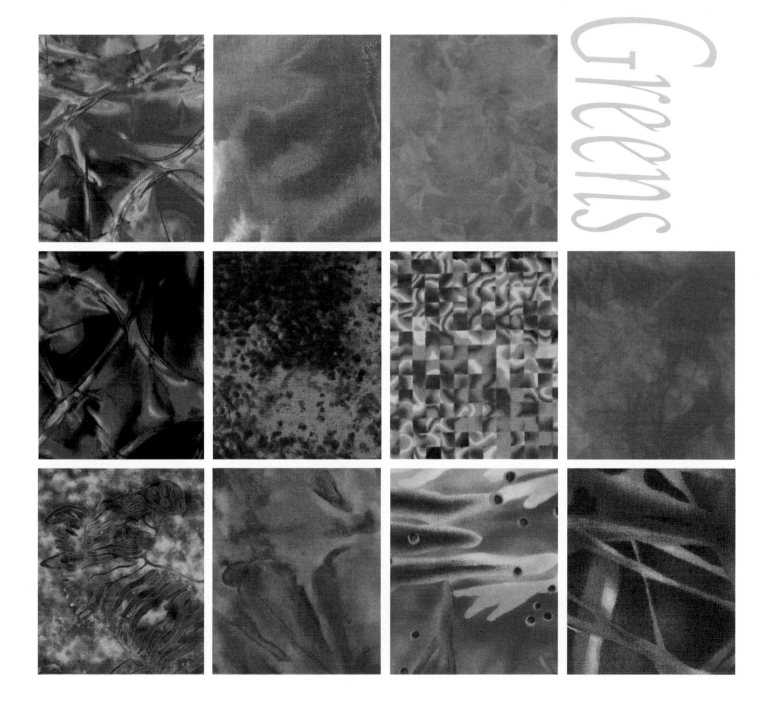

What about black and white? White has a tendency to expand and overflow its boundaries, affecting adjacent colors by creating a slightly washed out or tinted effect. Black achieves the opposite effect, letting each color display its own true sensation. Maybe that's why black and white together, with its reference to pop culture and graphic art, is such a versatile player and a staple in many fabric stashes. This color combination can be used for seemingly opposite purposes: to enhance a project's sophistication or to make it more playful.

White "light" pushes beyond the block edges. It's not necessarily wrong to put the viewer on edge, as long as it's deliberate.

Black & White

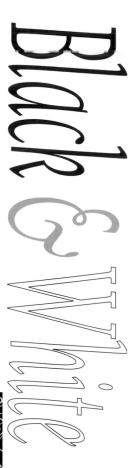

The term spreading effect refers to the way a color changes depending on what hues and fabrics it borders. The individual colors in this stripe take on completely different meanings when banded together in a stripe. Isolated from each other, their color personas would not be as vivid and clear.

Seemingly Seamless

In traditional patchwork, the visual key to the design is established by contrasting colors at the seams. A Nine-Patch, for example,

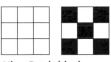

Nine-Patch block

features a single shape—the square—laid out in a checkerboard effect. For the audience to "see" the shapes, the quiltmaker chooses fabrics with contrasting colors or values to create a distinct, obvious line between patches 1 and 2.

My MO is often the opposite: to camouflage seams and create seemingly seamless connections. This encourages an uninterrupted flow of design or color from one patch to the next. Instead of sharp, straight edges defining geometric shapes, the result is a smooth transition from patch to patch, with the illusion that there is no seam at all.

To invent seamless connections, you have to free yourself from a conventional sense of patchwork. The trick is to choose a fabric based on the color in its background, the color that will land right along the seamline and connect to the neighboring patch's background color. That position, right at the seam, turns out to be crucial. When the color that functions as the ground in Patch 1 is pieced to a similar color in Patch 2, the seamline between them is disguised. Instead of focusing on the patchwork lines, we see patterns in the fabric advance and float against a receding common ground. This illusion is easier to pull off with dark rather than light backgrounds, because colors like black, indigo, forest green, and wine tend to blend smoothly into one another.

It's not that I never want to use a seamline to create an area of contrast. Rather, I plan these areas deliberately and judiciously, because I am aware of the role they play in the design. I don't hold it against quilt blocks that they are composed of geometric shapes. But often, to create a design brimming with elaborate details and interlaced patterns, I need to disguise the geometry that ultimately allows me to sew it all together.

The seamlines in this pieced block virtually disappear. See the original fabric on page 80.

That's why, when I hunt for the next fabric, the search is based on the relationship I want to establish with the previous fabric. Sometimes I want to continue the color, motif, or mood, with minimal contrast. Other times, I want to clearly define where one patch ends and the next begins. I find terms like *sharp* or *harsh, mild* or *minimal,* useful for defining degrees of contrast. This vocabulary focuses my options and directs the search.

So, in a nutshell, what is the quilter's quandary? To contrast or not to contrast, that is the question. Whether it is better to use distinct colors and end up with an obvious, visible seam that defines a geometric shape or to disguise the seam by placing similar colors at the seamline. It's as simple as that.

Common Ground

This next piecing strategy offers an alternate way of thinking about seamless connections. Consider a piece of patterned fabric as if it were a dimensional object. Make a distinction between what is figure (pattern) and what is ground. The goal is to establish the illusion of one continuous negative space by causing the backgrounds of neighboring patches to visually combine into a common ground. What reads from a distance as an integrated whole is discovered, on close inspection, to be a highly patched work.

You can reinvent a printed fabric's dark background. See the original fabric on page 55.

Figure and Ground

In a traditional patchwork block, the figure is the featured design and the ground is everything else. To read a pieced star, the viewer must be able to distinguish between the positive and negative shapes, between the figure and the ground. The star may be the subject and focal point of the composition, but equally important is the way the empty space is organized around it. Some of the most elegant patchwork blocks have a lot of important negative space.

Some fabrics step into patches and fill up the space snugly, like a pair of half-size-too-small jeans. They convey weight and mass. Other fabrics are always perceived as empty, negative space. When the design demands a full-figured focus alongside an unobtrusive ground, put the fabric patches on a design wall and step back to see how they decode in context.

The Butterfly Effect

Here's a painless way to tell if a fabric print is symmetrical. Imagine a butterfly. It has two wings and what I unscientifically call a "belly." A symmetrical print will have a similar structure: two "wings," filled with patterns, that are each other's mirror image and a "belly" (usually an itty-bitty motif), where one wing of fabric connects to the other.

If you have trouble finding the butterfly, start with the belly. In other words, look for an implied line down the middle of a motif that divides it into right and left halves. Check to see whether the pattern on one side of the line is the mirror image of the pattern on the other side. A design is considered a mirror image when it can be superimposed on itself by flipping it over.

Grown-up terms for the belly of a symmetrical design are the *central axis*, the *axis of symmetry*, or the *axis of reflection*. And the gussied-up term for the butterfly effect is *bilateral symmetry*, because it is formed of two sides, like the human body.

 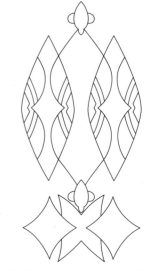

This symmetrical print illustrates the butterfly effect.

Outline drawing of the motif

Sea Foam

Why, in those glorious moments when we're lucky enough to find ourselves plunked down on a white sand beach, do we gaze, mesmerized by the sea, and think, "I could stare at this for hours." My theory? The staccato rhythm of foaming whitecaps compels the eyes to move around in a very satisfying way, searching for the next frothy swell. For some reason, the eternal ebb and flow of white meringues against a dark shimmering sea is simultaneously stimulating and soothing.

This discussion is about how to introduce that same satisfying brightness onto the flat surface of a quilt. Don't assume that using a light-colored fabric will do the trick. I've already explained how a light fabric placed next to a dark one will cause a blatant line of contrast. If you want to shed light onto your quilt, let light-colored motifs that stand out against appropriately colored backgrounds do it. Light colors splattered like randomly tossed confetti or churning like mermaid's breath rise from the quilt surface the way sea foam flits on top of cresting waves. It's your chance to both lighten up and energize the block.

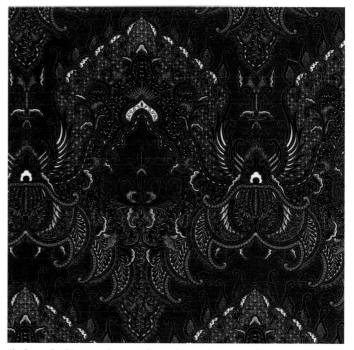

Flashes of white sea foam enliven this arabesque print.

The Kaleidoscope Legacy

For more than ten years, the state-of-the-art kaleidoscope has been both my design inspiration and my classroom. Analyzing what a scope is and what it isn't has steered me in lots of valuable directions. Becoming a kaleidoscope aficionado has made me more adaptable and flexible. The notion that there is no best, absolute, correct fabric selection is very liberating. After all, a breathtaking collision of color in a kaleidoscope will maneuver itself into something different in the instant it takes me to hand the scope to you.

Surprise. Magic. Change. Chance. To conjure the kaleidoscope personality and apply it to my quilting, I've learned to trust in symmetry, rely on detail, and believe that the whole will always be greater than the sum of its parts. No matter what direction my future quilts take, this personal design vocabulary, gleaned through the eyepiece of a kaleidoscope, will take the journey with me.

Bits of light, bright colors bubble up like whitecaps on the ocean. The effect is light and playful, even though the fabrics are predominantly dark.

What else have I learned? Since kaleidoscopes rely on the reflection of light rays from mirrors, the interior image always seems luminous. This incandescent view taught me to hoard fabrics that seem to emit self-generated light because they will generously lend this light to my design.

I've also learned that fabrics don't have to match. Focus on matching seams, not colors. Perfectly matched colors can be boring, while comparable colors that bear a resemblance to each other create more sophisticated connections. An unconventional combination of fabrics simulates the appealing and random nature of a kaleidoscope. If you want to stick to a color family, be flexible. If something catches your eye, try it. You might not like every result, but the opportunity to self-critique has its rewards. What's the worst that can happen? You turn on NPR, and you rip.

Fabric with luminous glow

On Grain vs. In a Girdle

In the best of all possible blocks, the patches along the perimeter are cut on-grain. But sometimes we fancy a slanting stripe or a wandering paisley. As long as stability is provided by the final boundary, you can discipline interior off-grain patches to behave.

Staystitching is one way to add stability to off-grain edges (so I've been told). But an idea I like even better is to girdle the block with on-grain strips that exert firm control. The girdle solution raises a color question: whether to

continue the already established hues and blur the transition, so the girdle isn't noticeable, or to choose a contrasting color, so the girdle functions like a frame. Think of the second scenario as a chance to use even more fabric.

Of course, any block that's headed into a traditional quilt setting is going to bump into sashing, which, when cut on-grain, will stabilize any unruly block behavior.

Details, Details, Details

With the type of template making I'm going to teach you, you could plop an entire motif in a patch—but would you want to? Do you really want to slow down the action and give the audience time to identify butterflies fluttering in the middle of your block, or do you want them to experience the gestalt? Sometimes, like when you're making placemats for that friend who's moving from Jersey City to open a diner in Buffalo, Wyoming, you want a bevy of line-dancing cowgirls. But more often than not, a recognizable image multiplied many times equals predictable, which translates to boring. Multiplying a fragment, on the other hand, yields a unique, imaginative bit of intricacy that never existed before. Because it is unexpected, the effect is more spontaneous, less contrived.

Faux Curves

A line is a series of points. But one day, my perspective on this fact reversed and led me to a brand-new skill. Instead of connecting points to make a line, I could draw any line and break it up into points. This means that if I use a compass to draft a circle in my quilt block diagram, I can then reform it into straight lines using a ruler. If I mark those lines on the corresponding template and find a fabric motif that mimics the line, the resulting image will appear to be as complete and accurate a circle as the compass-drawn one. The straight-pretending-to-be-circular lines don't have to be continuous from patch to patch. The eye is kind enough to connect them into a pleasing loop even when it skips stops. An alternate option is to mark a curve on the template and then use the see-through template to find a motif with an identical curve (see Block 1F, page 56).

Fabric motifs with curves form a circle. See the original fabric on page 65.

The Design Process

This next discussion is about the fact that it takes longer than you expect to design something good. Designing doesn't proceed along a straight line. It goes forward and back and wanders around in all directions. It's not always a fun place to be. Sometimes the "aha" moments arrive unbidden via cartoonish lightbulbs. Other times you just have to hunker down and coax inspiration. When I've plodded away in an unproductive place way too long, the act of doing something different, of focusing on one small task, calms me down.

Typically, when I am stuck, I dive headfirst into piles of fabrics. It's kind of a Zen thing. Enlightenment is attained by pretending to organize while really I'm hunting and gathering. I grab the fabrics that ask to be in the current project even if they seem like unlikely guests. They've touched some intuitive link in my brain, and like a CSI agent, my job is to investigate every option. Usually this problem-solving effort becomes a creative springboard, giving rise to what-if scenarios that lead to unexpectedly delightful results. At least, that's how I do it. Think for a minute. You use problem-solving skills every day. You know your own idiosyncratic way to rev those skills into high gear.

Be patient. Don't accept a solution if you don't like it. (If you don't like it now, you won't like it when the quilt is finished.) It takes a long time to make something good. In fact, it takes all kinds of time: looking time, musing time, auditioning time, screwing-up time, constructing and deconstructing time. Give yourself the luxury of time to harvest those valuable what-if ideas. It's a terrible thing to waste a great idea, the kind that matures as the project develops.

I need an eclectic mix of multitalented fabrics. It is, after all, my palette. Whether fabrics belong to different styles or are intrinsically compatible is not an issue for me. I practice "pieceful" coexistence. I love fabrics that tickle my imagination: designs with hyperabundant colors and charismatic patterns, prints that play well with both commercial and dyed stuff, textiles that sometimes set the stage and sometimes dance on it. I want it all, I want it now, and I make no excuses for the size of my stash. Architect Robert Venturi's postmodern maxim "less is a bore" echoes my sentiments exactly. As I have often said, I feel sorry for the ones who don't get it.

Over the years, I've developed a vocabulary to describe the personality and function of the fabrics I use. This personal lexicon divides fabrics into two categories: prima donnas and allovers.

The Prima Donnas

Prima donnas are powerful design elements. Simultaneously temperamental and charismatic, they are the divas that give a design its distinctive voice. Any fabric that is composed of motifs that are the exact duplicates of one another is a prima donna. Quilters call them "fussy cuts" because creating lots of identical patches requires effort. These high-maintenance fabrics need to be lavished with attention, but they always pay off.

Symmetrical Fabric

The fussiest prima donnas are symmetrical, like a butterfly (see The Butterfly Effect on page 16). A bilaterally symmetrical motif can be divided into identical halves by a line passing through the center. The layout is a mirror repeat, from left to right and sometimes from top to bottom.

Once you get to know them, symmetrical fabrics aren't very intimidating at all. Intricate designs arranged in ordered layouts are as invaluable as they are provocative. They challenge me to stretch and invent clever patchwork to maximize their graceful behaviors. You'll grow to covet these clever and versatile illusion makers because, in the end, you will get credit for the work that they do.

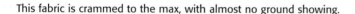

This fabric is crammed to the max, with almost no ground showing.

This fabric has two axes of symmetry, one vertical and one horizontal.

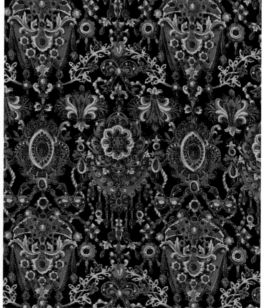

Lots of small, densely spaced motifs increase the design options.

Symmetrical motifs are usually printed on-grain, but there are lots of sightings of the off-the-straight-of-grain variety, too.

21

Pseudosymmetricals

Some motifs give the appearance of symmetry at first glance, but a closer inspection reveals differences between the two sides. I call these fabrics pseudosymmetricals. You want to be able to recognize a symmetrical wannabe when you see one and learn what it can and cannot do.

You can use pseudosymmetrical patches in a block to imitate symmetry as long as the patches don't touch one another. The eye will interpret the rhythmic repetition of elements as symmetrical even if the motifs are a little lopsided. Small discrepancies will not be noticed. The problem arises when you try to sew two pseudosymmetrical patches to one another in mirror image. If the two sides of the motif are different, even just a little bit, they won't connect seamlessly, no matter how hard you try.

To detect an imposter, trace hints from the motif on template plastic. Flip the plastic over onto the assumed mirror image motif to see if the hints line up in exactly the same way.

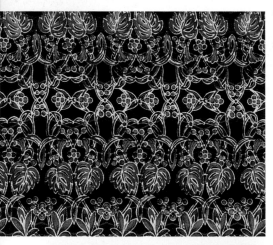

These mirror image motifs are loosely rendered and result in discrepancies between the left side and the right.

The two halves of each pineapple leaf motif do not make an identical match.

Mirror Image Motifs

Symmetrical fabrics aren't our only source of mirror image patches. Some fabrics contain individual mirror image motifs, such as butterflies, within a larger free-style design. Another option is paired motifs, such as paisleys, but be careful—these can be deceptive. What seems to be a pair of mirror image figures, one wiggling left and the other wiggling right, often turns out to be the same motif oriented identically in only one direction. It's one and the same figure rendered right side up and then upside down without actually being flipped over.

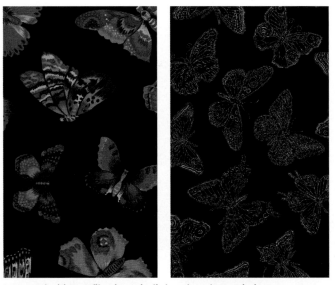

Symmetrical butterflies have built-in mirror image halves.

 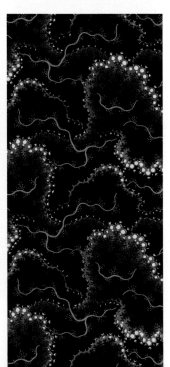

Right- and left-facing motifs abound in these fabrics.

Classic Stripes

Stripes automatically slide the eye from here to there, forming visual pathways that instill an element of motion. One-way stripes have a distinct top and bottom and must be oriented in the same direction, but two-way stripes can be turned upside down or right side up, and no one would notice. Either kind of stripe can be printed or woven.

Realize that there's more than one way to piece a stripe. The effects are completely different if you cut parallel or perpendicular (or even diagonal) to the selvage, so audition which way you want the stripe positioned in the patch. Sketching the options on a graph paper diagram or a graphless mini version (see Block Diagrams to Photocopy on page 94) helps me decide. Stripes can become fussy cuts, and sometimes they are good candidates to use randomly.

Just like vertical stripes make a body seem taller and horizontal stripes emphasize its width, a striped fabric in a patchwork block accentuates the direction it travels, sometimes creating the illusion that a square block is wider than it is tall.

Woven stripes

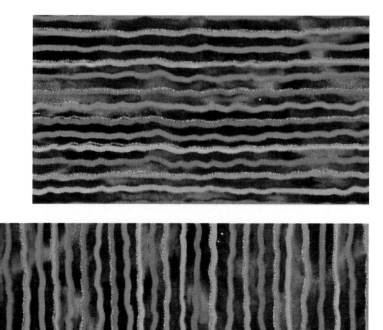

Decide which way you want the stripes to run: horizontally or vertically.

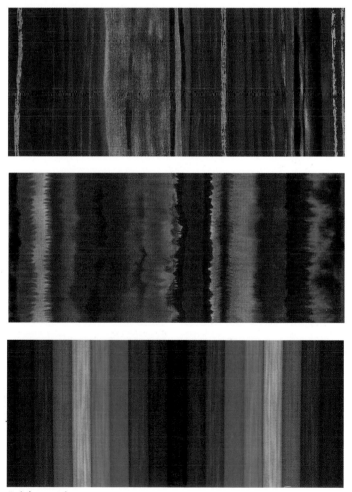
Rainbow stripes

23

Wacky Stripes

Now is the time to expand your definition of stripes. Add function to your definition of this form. We're going to include any linear textile pattern that is capable of steering visual traffic, no matter how wide, wiggly, or irregular the bands.

Wacky stripes, as I call them, do have certain limitations. Zigzags and serpentine stripes infuse a lively quality, but their erratic behavior sometimes makes it difficult to create the illusion of a continuous line from patch to patch, especially in fairly small patches. Historically, undulating stripes were more commonly seen in the eighteenth and nineteenth centuries; the twentieth century's prejudice against snakelike patterns made them unfashionable and unpopular. I guess it can be disconcerting when a design intended for apparel seems sinuous and writhing. But most of the time, a wavy stripe is just a device that offers a strong sense of movement and the opportunity to achieve a playful optical effect.

A classic stripe can be used randomly along the same color band because any portion can visually substitute for another. But if you cut a wacky stripe into segments, every arbitrary segment won't necessarily line up neatly into a seemingly continuous row. A fussy cut of the exact same or similar segment of the stripe is usually needed in order to visually connect from patch to patch.

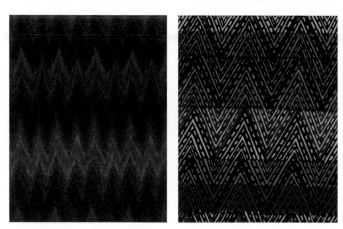

Zigzag stripes

 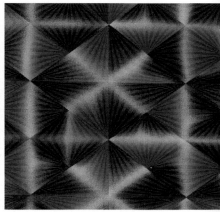

A figure surprinted on a striped background

Diagonal stripes

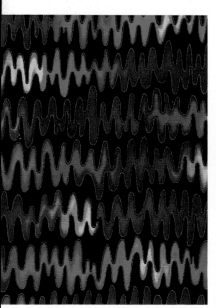

Wavy stripes

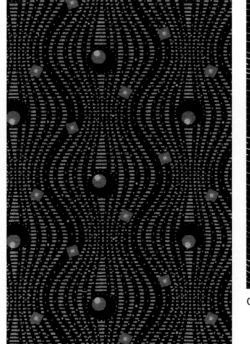

Curvy stripes

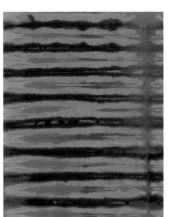
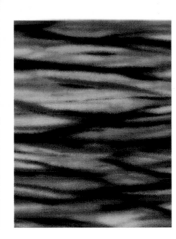
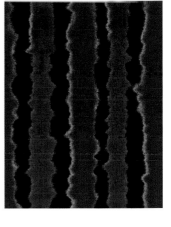

Batik and pretend batik stripes

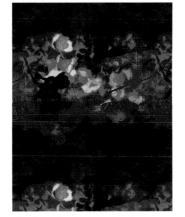
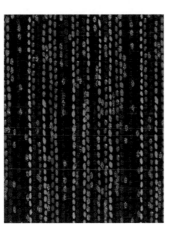

Shadowy background stripes   Pointillist stripes   Marbleized stripes

A directional pattern with noteworthy shading or pattern gradation makes an imaginative choice for sashing or anywhere you need to create visual pathways.

Ombré is the textile designer's term for colors that gradually shade and blend into another color. This adept transition from light to dark or subtle change from one color into another adds complexity while carrying the viewer's eye smoothly from one form to the next. Attaching a shadow to a basic stripe sets off vibrations that pop the stripe off a fabric's flat surface.

Ombré

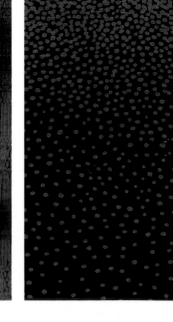

Ombré effects

Novelty Prints

When you cross over into my way of using fabric, your vision alters. You'll find yourself seeking the unexpected, the fabric you wouldn't normally buy. Novelty prints offer fantastic palette and design possibilities, once you know what you're looking for. The idea is to concentrate on the details of a fabric's interior and ignore its total effect. Paradoxically, this narrow perspective widens the selection. The secondary components of a print take on an active life of their own.

Tip **Prints that depict subjects from nature are often rendered with painterly qualities. The shadings and highlights in this type of printed cloth will add a quality of shifting light to your mini masterpiece.**

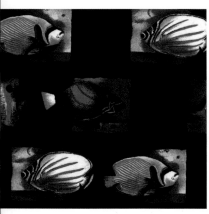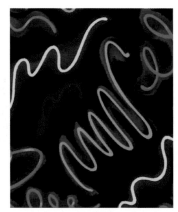

Novelty prints

Symbiotic Fabric

Some fabrics don't look like much on their own, but when attached to other fabrics, they add pizzazz. There's a surprising mutual benefit to the relationship. One fabric accessorizes the other. Sometimes just a snippet of the unassuming fabric helps you achieve an elegant, seamless outcome. See Block 6D (page 85).

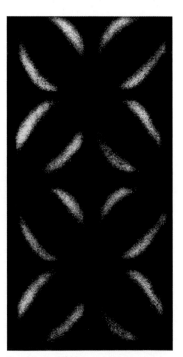

Symbiotic fabric

HOW MUCH TO BUY?

When buying a prima donna, keep in mind that odd-shaped, off-grain patches can spread across two repeats, requiring double the amount, especially when the repeats are close together. I usually end up buying 1 yard of a small repeat and at least 2 yards of a big one. When you find highly stylized arabesque motifs set far apart, you'll feel like you're buying acreage in order to guarantee enough repeats, but the potential for mesmerizing designs makes it worth the investment.

I buy ½- to 1-yard cuts of allovers. I know I will always be seduced by the novelty of new ones, and I'll want to buy them all.

Allovers

Allovers play a vital supporting role. Compared with the fussy prima donna, they are versatile and noncomplaining. The nondirectional design of the allover looks the same from any angle. There is no implicit top, bottom, left, or right. Patches are easy to cut, and the fabric is perfect for strip piecing. I've identified several categories of allovers to suit my piecing needs.

Prints

We don't usually notice the layout or pattern of allover prints. The typical print contains more figure than ground, and at first glance or when viewed from a distance, it may even appear to be a solid. An alternate set spaces motifs more widely apart, exposing lots of background. A third option combines both. In one area, the design is sparse and loosely packed, then a few inches over, it crams together in a congested crowd. This type of print creates a lively, spontaneous effect when used randomly, as long as the patches relate to one another in some way.

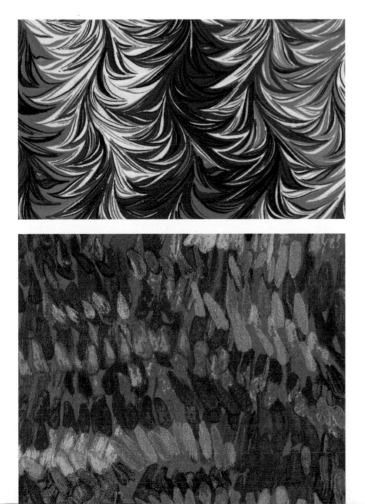

Dots and Dashes

Fabrics printed with lots of colors in a tiny area energize the most disheartened design. Think dots. I like when dots go bonkers, splattering into colored patterns of randomly tossed speckles, like confetti. Dots organized in a sequential pattern cause the viewer's eye to play connect-the-dots, sparking a dynamic quality. Make the dots a little longer, and you've got dashes.

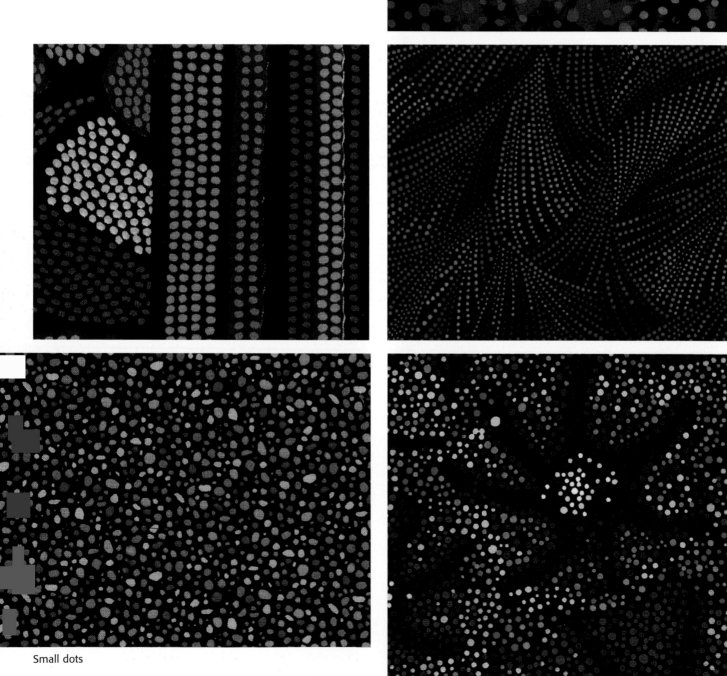

Small dots

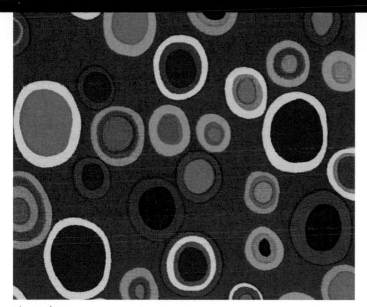

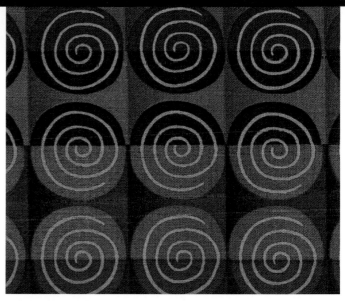

Bigger dots

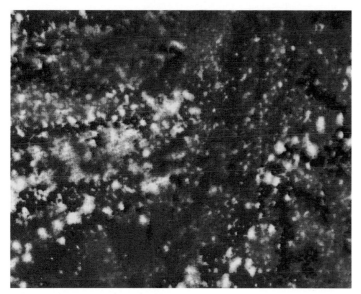

Splattered dots

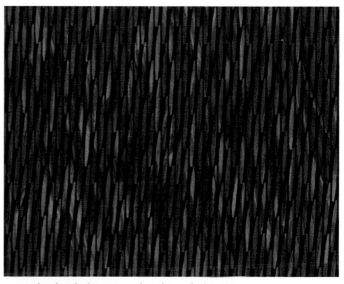

Dashes

Long, slender dashes. Note that these dashes move in one direction.

Reads Like a Solid

For the record, I never use true solids. It seems as if I am eternally hunting for specimens crammed with an abundance of shading. The "reads like a solid" fabric often becomes a source of luminosity. A finished product that seems dimensional is always more interesting than one that reads as virtually flat.

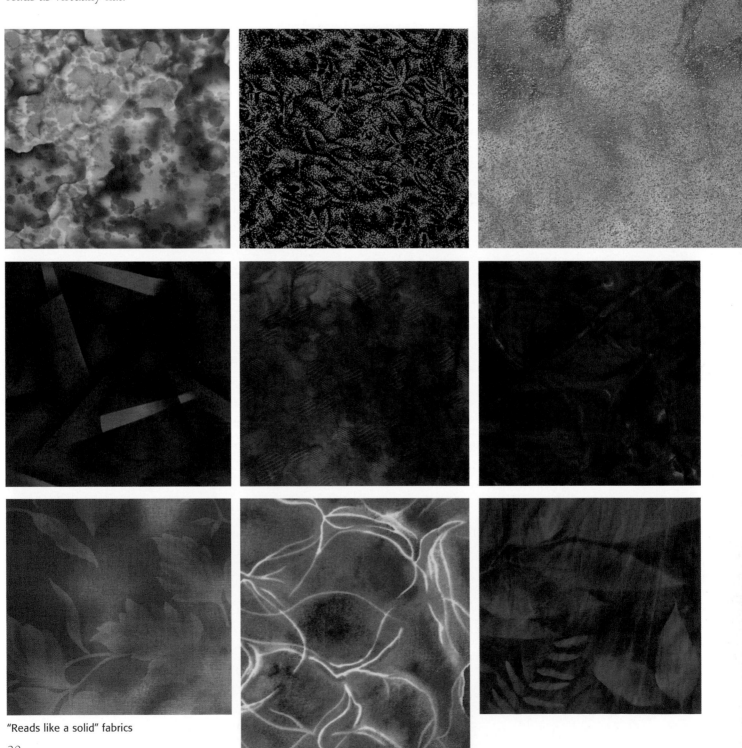

"Reads like a solid" fabrics

Clever Fabric Tricks

The Two-Faced Batik

Part of a batik's appeal is its relaxed, handmade look. Clearly, we would not expect reliable mirror images from these exotic, primitive motifs. Surprise! Batiks are reversible! Because of the dye process, the figures are often equally legible on both sides of the fabric. Usually, you can't tell the right from the wrong side; slight color shifts between the designated front and back can usually be ignored. If you have bears lumbering westward, turn the fabric over and they'll be heading east.

The Not-So-Sensuous Silk

The luminous colors of pure silk are simply irresistible. I turn silk fabrics from slippery into stable by pressing fusible woven interfacing onto the back. Once the silk is relieved of its free-flowing drape, it strips and pieces just like a crisp cotton.

Search in fabric shops geared to apparel makers for the most featherweight fusible available. If you hand quilt, test how the interfacing needles. Some fusible adhesives strip the thread or impede the needle's piercing action.

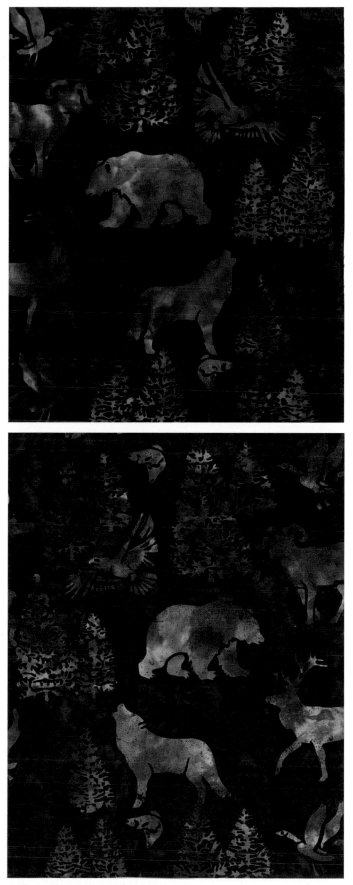

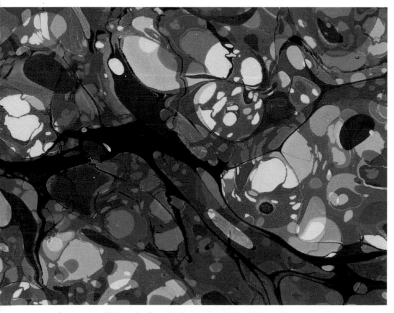

A lustrous silk backed with lightweight fusible adhesive will handle like a cotton. Silk hand marbled by Cosette Marbled Silks, Austin, Texas.

Batik motifs, coming and going

The Versatile Stripe

Think of a striped layout as bands of color stripped together. Now focus on the demarcation between two colored bands, because this line will be responsible for the magic that follows. Decide where the stripe should fall in the patch. I usually audition positions by sketching possibilities in a small facsimile of the block. Place the line in an unexpected way, not necessarily so that the stripes are evenly distributed in the design.

Mark the selected line on the template. Since the line imitates a seamline but represents the boundary between two color bands, it can create the effect of a narrow strip without a bulky seam. Again, the stripe doesn't have to be horizontal, vertical, or evenly distributed. You can use this technique to work in slim, conspicuous jabs of new color or to mimic a curve. Remember that in a pair of mirror image patches, the direction of the stripe must be reversed.

The Artistic License

When it comes to making a quilt, letting go of traditional practices—meaning the way pioneer women did it—isn't cheating. It's innovative. Do you have an overpowering element staring you in the face? Muffle it with an appliqué or embroider a few stitches or add a few beads to create a more graceful transition. Promise me you'll never call it cheating when you use a permanent marker to conceal some leftover particles of pattern that refused to get buried in the seam. Or let's say you find the perfect motif, but because the shape it has to fit into is a tad too big, extraneous stuff piggybacks on it, tainting the view. Doesn't it seem clever to color over these misguided discrepancies? Go ahead. You're the designer. The block is yours. Who are you misleading? The aforementioned preindustrial foremothers? Do you really think those make-do women would begrudge you a few clever, newfangled fixes?

Block 6E. To decode the stripe placement, see page 68.

Templating

There is a time and a place for templates, and that time is now. In recent years, templates have gotten a bad rap, perhaps because they've been banned from the wide world of quick quilts. But I give templates a lot of credit for leading me places I could not get to on my own. Without them, I am powerless. With them, I become Super Quilter, able to leap tall piles of fabric in a single bound, to contort myself like a rubbery super hero, to explore fabric from every possible angle without leaving my seat.

When I first set eyes on an intricately patterned fabric, I see the whole design laid out the way it was styled, typically in a top-to-bottom, left-to-right orientation. With the second glance, my mind's eye gets to work, skipping about, exploring off-kilter and absurd angles, trying to isolate fragments of the pattern and predict which ones might morph into something spectacular when joined with other fabrics in the block du jour. I'm not only looking for distinctive motifs to center in the patch. My focus is simultaneously aimed toward the seamline.

Why care about what lands at the seamline? Because in some patchwork scenarios, the motif that winds up along the seamline connects to its mirror image or joins forces with a different motif to continue the design into the next patch. Other times, you want a motif to float elegantly against a common ground. Here, you search for a next-door fabric with the same ground color along the seamline that is in the first patch's background. Each case results in a camouflaged connection. Seamlines disappear, intricacy reigns, and you get credit for the magic (even when you are just as surprised by the results as everyone else).

But enough talk. Sounding clairvoyant about a fabric's star potential means diddly-squat. Getting a motif to step with precision into a specific shape and replicating it exactly multiple times—now, that's the impressive feat. To pull it off, we turn to the transparent template.

Tip The process you are about to learn is template-driven. Using transparent template material and marking the seam allowance on it gives you a template that functions like a window. This frame allows you to identify the area of the fabric that will be visible in the patch. You can see, in advance, what part of the fabric bumps into the seamline.

A Puzzling, Perplexing Purple Piece of Patchwork to Ponder, 2004, 50″ × 66″, designed, machine pieced, and machine quilted by Deborah Tilley. See the quilt diagram with block placement on page 50.

Tools of the Trade

The truth is, I don't really sew very well. But I want it to look like I do. Fabricating this illusion means using simple, reliable tools consistently, from the beginning of a project to the end. All of your measuring devices (rulers, graph paper, template plastic) must agree with each other. Otherwise, no matter how carefully you've measured your pieces, they still might not fit together. Here's what you'll need:

- **Graph paper**: Choose an 8-to-the-inch grid with bold inch lines. The bold inch lines make the grid easier to read and allow you to use it as a ruler. Buy sheets big enough to accommodate the 12″ × 12″ finished size of the blocks in this book.

- **See-through template plastic**: Template plastic is available plain or with a grid. A grid serves as a ruler and helps tame symmetrical motifs. Clear plastic makes it easier to see through to the fabric underneath. You usually get four 8½″ × 10¾″ sheets in a package. Do not purchase long sheets that are rolled and sold in a tube. You could flatten these under your mattress for a year and they'll curl right back into a roll as soon as they make their escape.

- **C-Thru Ruler**

- **Extra-fine-point permanent markers**: You'll use these to mark thin lines on both templates and fabrics. My favorite pen is the difficult-to-find Pilot Extra Fine Point Permanent Marker, SCA-UF. It leaves a thin, visible line on the template and glides smoothly without stretching the fabric. No matter which pen you choose, the line width is key. If the line is too thin, you'll waste time trying to find it. If it's too plump, your patches and templates will increase in size and lose accuracy.

- **Gel ink pens**: You need a way to mark thin, permanent, visible cutting (not sewing) lines on dark-colored fabrics.

I used to use white chalk pencils, which required constant sharpening. Then I discovered these newfangled light-colored, acid-free permanent gel ink pens. Pick a color with the potential for glaring visibility: a neon pastel or glittery silver.

- **Fabric scissors**

- **Paper and plastic template scissors**: Get the picture? One scissors for fabric, another scissors for paper and plastic. Always use separate scissors for separate tasks.

- **Rotary cutter, ruler, and mat**: For trimming patches, I use the Brooklyn Revolver, which is a circular rotary mat mounted on a lazy Susan, and a small 30mm rotary cutter.

How to Get Started

Draft the complete block its actual size in pencil on graph paper. This diagram functions as your ongoing, work-in-progress blueprint. It provides an accurate outline from which to make precise templates, plus it's the design plan that explains the relationship between the patches. Miniature facsimiles of the six blocks used in this book are on page 94.

Tip Okay, I admit it. What if gel ink pens turn out to be hole-causing time bombs? Here's my defense: A gel pen doesn't bleed, and since you cut fabric patches by aiming straight down the middle of the marked line, most of the line disappears anyway. Should anything go chemically wrong a hundred years from now, there's barely any residue to wreak havoc on the fabric. In the meantime, you're able to see the line, enjoy the process, feel successful, and keep blood pressure down. These are all good perks.

How to Make a Template

No matter how complex a shape is, the technique for making a template is always the same. Let's say we want to make a template for Patch 1 in Block 1. You've already drafted the complete block at its actual size on graph paper. Lay a sheet of template plastic on the graph paper diagram, over Patch 1, with enough margin to add a ¼″ seam allowance all around. Use a ruler and permanent pen to trace the patch outline onto the template plastic. Make sure the lines are dark and legible but not fat. Use the permanent pen to make every mark on a template.

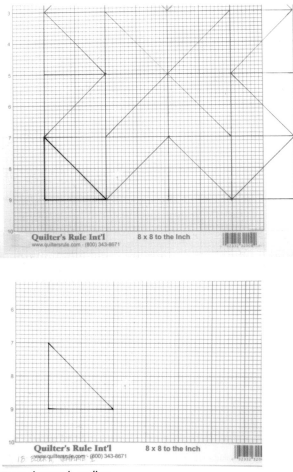

Trace the patch outline.

Next, add a ¼″ seam allowance. For this task, I use the top edge of a C-Thru Ruler, the side without the logo. On an 8-to-the-inch grid ruler, two lines equal ¼″. Align the ruler's ¼″ delineation on the edge of the patch so that ¼″ of the ruler extends beyond the patch and the rest of the ruler rests on the patch. Simply zip a line along the ruler edge. Do this all around.

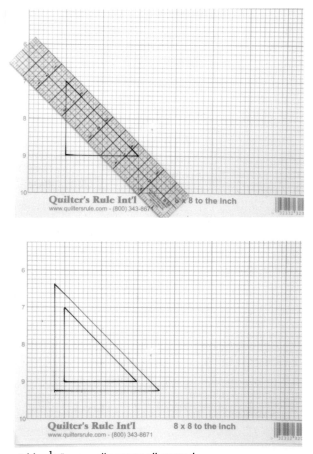

Add a ¼″ seam allowance all around.

Cut out the template, aiming down the center of the marked line. The objective is to maintain, not increase or decrease, the size of a template that you will use to cut multiple identical patches. I use scissors, but use a rotary cutter if it is your cutting gizmo of choice.

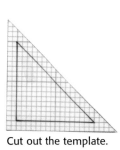

Cut out the template.

Symmetrical Templates

A symmetrical template is a template that can be divided into identical halves by a line passing through its center. It is reversible, reading the same from left to right or right to left. To make a symmetrical template more functional, use template plastic with a grid and align a bold line of the grid directly on the midline of the patch. This simple strategy ensures an accurate, bilaterally symmetrical, left-right orientation. Marking the shape at random, without regard for the bold lines, cancels out the grid's purpose and may actually confuse you.

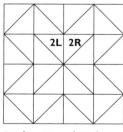

A symmetrical template with centered bold lines

Mirror Image Templates

Mirror image patches require special attention when it comes to making templates. In Block 1, patches 2L and 2R are the mirror image of one another. Each shape is a non-reversible and asymmetrical patch. To obtain an accurate mirror image of such a shape, simply flip over the see-through template. In other words, to cut all twelve patch 2's, you need to make only one template. Use it first to mark six 2L patches, then flip it over and use it wrong side up to mark six 2R patches. Sharing the same template is more accurate than making two templates for each pair of mirror image patches.

Patches 2L and 2R form a mirror image pair.

Marking directional cues on asymmetrical templates becomes an important reference system. With many shapes, you'll find the orientation is not immediately obvious once the template is cut out. Without some sort of marking, you risk placing a template topsy-turvy on the carefully selected fabric motif or cutting twelve patches in one direction. To help me orient the template to the block pattern, I mark "L + R" at the top of the template. When I pick up the template, I automatically know which end is up because the cues are toward the top. When the letters are legible, I know the template is aligned to the left side. When the template is flipped over and the letters are reversed, I know the template is aligned to the right side.

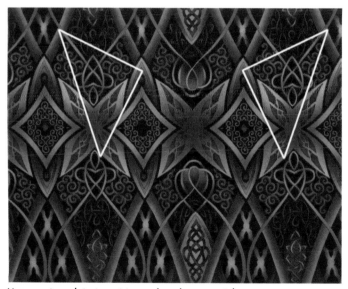

Use one template to cut two mirror image patches.

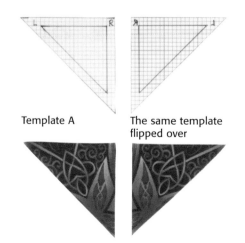

Template A · The same template flipped over

When Template Meets Fabric

Place the windowlike template on the front of the fabric. Move it a teensy bit to the right to catch a shadowy beam; tweak it to the left to include a curl. Move it up, move it down, turn it upside down, rotate it off grain. Let the template take you into nooks and crannies that didn't seem interesting before. Here is your chance to catch some curves or to spray some sea foam. If the potential for seemingly endless possibilities overwhelms you, keep this thought in mind: There is no correct or best selection. What you pick today may be different from what you would pick tomorrow.

Move the template around on the fabric.

Don't guess whether two patches have the ability to relate. Audition links between a patch and its prospective neighbor by physically placing potential fabrics against the original patch's seamline. Promise me you won't take it personally if this search for the perfect motif takes a long time. Become the patient little search engine that can. Your mind's eye learns an awful lot during this quest, even while receiving angst-ridden messages that the process is taking way too long and it's all your fault. Sometimes, to get from a boring "here" to an inspired "there," you have to make a lot of stops in between.

When you work with bilaterally symmetrical templates, make sure mirror image doohickeys land identically from left to right. Use the bold line down the middle of the template to divide the design into identical halves. Use the grid to verify that the fabric is evenly distributed to the left and right of the midpoint. Pick a doodad, identify its position to the left of the center, and then check to see if its mirror image lands in the corresponding position to the right. It's fabric, not wood. It stretches. Go ahead and give it a little tug to encourage it into alignment.

THE LAWS OF FABRIC GRAIN

Patchwork tradition recommends that all patches be cut on-grain to promote stable blocks that lie nice and flat. I admit this is a truly reasonable principle. In fact, in a small book published in 1991, I wrote, "The maximum number of straight edges of the template should be parallel to the straight grain of the fabric."

Since then, beguiled by countless patterns, I've evolved into a nonpurist. My MO is to wiggle my template into every tempting, lopsided pose possible in order to catch the just-right motif. What can I say? I've become a material girl.

I use my template in this catawampus, no-regard-for-grain way only for fussy cuts, not for allovers. Unless I'm trying to catch the just-right shades in a multihued batik (see Block 5D, page 79), allovers are usually strip pieced (see Strip Piecing/Power Stitching, page 46) or cut following strict rules of grain. I count on on-grain allovers to stabilize a patchwork assembled from a mix of on-grain and off-grain pieces.

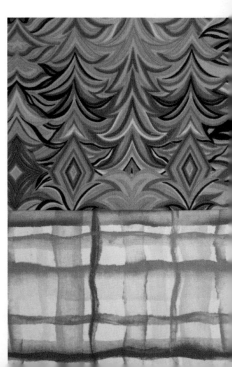

Auditioning links

How to Mark a Template

Once you've decided where to position the template on the fabric, hold it in place and use the permanent marker to trace details of the selected motif directly onto the template. I like to copy quite a bit of the motif—not just registration marks—because this helps me identify which motif I'm searching for. Lots of marks will help you find identical patches multiple times. Choose distinctive eye-catching clues, the kind that will identify the position quickly and accurately. Attach names or labels to motifs so they get fixed in your memory and are easier to find: "Where is that bottle green Ninja turtle? Those ruby red Betty Boop lips?"

Let some of your markings spill across the seamlines into the seam allowance. Since this is where the actual matching and sewing takes place, this step facilitates accuracy at the seams.

Marking a template

How to Mark the Fabric

The fabric is marked on the front. If you're used to marking the back of the fabric, marking the front may not seem kosher. I mark the front so I can see the motifs clearly and recognize identical segments effortlessly and precisely. Use the clues marked on the template to superimpose the template on the corresponding motifs on the fabric's front side. Trace around the edge of the template with a permanent marker or a light-colored gel pen. To mark additional identical patches, align the template on the next available motif and repeat the process.

Occasionally, a line you mark will be indistinguishable from a fabric's printed design lines. If this ever happens to you, turn the fabric over to see if the line is recognizable from the wrong side. If it is, you can try marking that side instead. (If you do end up marking an asymmetrical template on the wrong side of the fabric, be sure to flip the template over, too. Two wrongs make a right.)

Marking fabric

How to Cut the Fabric

Here's where personality determines the process. If you are a rotary cutting connoisseur, go for it. You probably ignored the previous step, How to Mark the Fabric, since your plan is to place the template on the fabric and rotary cut around it. Otherwise, find a scissor that fits your hand and hide it from the rest of your family when you're not using it. Cut out the patch, aiming down the center of the marked line. The objective is to maintain, not increase or decrease, the size of the patch. If you are cutting out lots of identical patches from a prima donna, you'll end up with a holey fabric. Consider yourself blessed.

Behavior Problems

Bowing

If you haven't already experienced it, I'm sorry to be the one to warn you about an annoying fabric irregularity. Here's the scene: You have accurately marked a bunch of identical patches on a fabric with an obvious regular repeat, when suddenly the next one or two or three patches misbehave and refuse to line up with the template. You end up wondering if you imagined they lined up in the first place and immediately assume you are doing something wrong.

According to some garmentos I know, the culprit turns out to be a fabric predisposition called bowing. The problem is in the fabric right from the start, in its days as greige (pronounced "gray") goods. The term *greige goods* refers to the raw, untreated base cloth that comes off a loom, before anything is done to it. Bowing occurs when the fabric's warp and weft do not run perpendicular to each other and remain true to the selvage. It can easily be seen in a plaid when the fabric is ripped from selvage to selvage. The tear line isn't straight and dips by several inches.

Some element of bowing is to be expected. A good mill will attempt to minimize the effect as much as possible during the greige goods, preparatory, and finishing stages. Once the fabric is printed, significant bowing cannot be remedied. My ability to compensate for this distortion is based more on trial and error than fabric science. Here are my remedies, in order of usage.

1. Try to gently push and pull the fabric into alignment. Go ahead. It's fabric, not wood. It stretches. Maybe you can manipulate it into alignment.

2. See if a different row of the repeat will agree to line up with the template. This option is feasible only if you have ample fabric.

3. Figure out which fabric edges really bump into themselves. Those are the ones that have to be meticulously aligned. Line up the template, beginning with the essential edge and letting the others fall where they will. You can tolerate some distortion along edges that aren't destined to meet an identical twin.

4. Cut out a slightly larger piece than needed, block it with steam, and go for a rematch.

The Match Game

When you join a square to a square or a half-square triangle to another half-square triangle, the patches and angles being joined are the same. But sometimes, even though the two patches that need to be stitched along a common seam are the same shape, corners with different angles abut each other. The problem for us is that the techniques learned in traditional patchwork—match the edges and corners and then stitch—don't work when shapes with different angles are patched together. We don't care what the angles are; we just want them to fit together effortlessly.

This predicament exists in Block 6 (page 91). Align templates J1 and J2, with right sides together and Side a to Side b.

Uh-oh, there's a problem. The angles at the two point X's are different. Ditto for the point Y's. When you align the cut edges of two different angles, the resulting patch is distorted. No guideline exists to help you accurately position the fabric shapes together. Never assume they match "enough." Templates either match each other, or they don't. Estimating is not a viable option. We need foolproof.

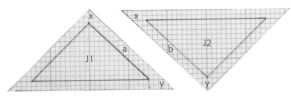

Angles at points X and Y do not match.

SOLUTION 1

Use this method when you have two templates to align.

1. Make templates 1 and 2 as usual.
2. Place the templates right sides together, as you would two fabric patches for seaming. Align the sewing lines and match points X and Y at each end. Once the two templates are precisely aligned, look closely at the template plastic in the vicinity of point X. See how a little triangle of extra plastic on Template 2 sticks out beyond Template 1? I have no idea why, but I call these tidbits of template that peek past a significant other *dog-ears*.
3. Using the rigid edge of Template 1 as a guide, mark and trim off the excess dog-ear.
4. Repeat steps 2 and 3, this time addressing the area around point Y. This finishing step is important. An accurate match must extend from cut edge to cut edge. Otherwise, when you are sitting at the sewing machine aligning two patches right sides together just before you sew them, you won't know what to aim for and can end up stretching a patch too much or not enough. The templates are now ready for you to cut fabric patches that will piece together flawlessly.

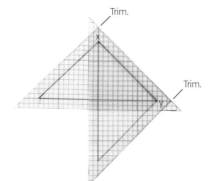

Use rigid edges of templates to trim the points.

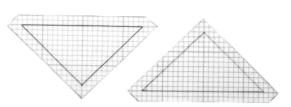

Trimmed templates are ready to use to cut fabric patches that will piece together perfectly.

SOLUTION 2

Use this method when you have only one template to work with, as in Block 6E (page 86). Although this block's rainbow effect necessitated fussy cutting, every patch was cut the same way. If you need only one template, why cut two? On the other hand, if only one template exists, how can you line up a template to itself? To find your way out of this conundrum, you'll need the full-size paper diagram (I prefer graph paper), the template, a ruler, and a permanent marker. You will be trimming the template to the diagram.

1. Focus on one of the shapes in the graph paper diagram. This shape corresponds to a single patch in the completed block. The outline of the shape represents the seamline. Now, if this seamline had a ¼″ seam allowance added to it—the way templates do—you could use the diagram to trim the plastic template. Use a pencil with a sharp point and a ruler to draw a perfectly accurate ¼″ seam allowance around this shape on your graph paper diagram.

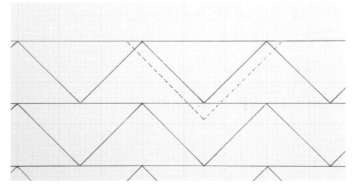

Mark a ¼″ seam allowance on the diagram (shown here as a red dash line).

2. Turn over the plastic template and place it on the diagram, right sides together, as if you were going to sew the two shapes together. See the little triangle of plastic that extends beyond the seam allowance? Using the seam allowance line as a guide, mark a corresponding line on the template with a permanent marker. Trim off this protruding tip.

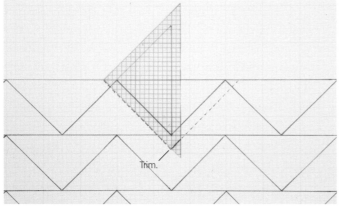

Trim the point to match the seam allowance.

3. Rotate the template 180° and repeat step 2 to trim the other tip.

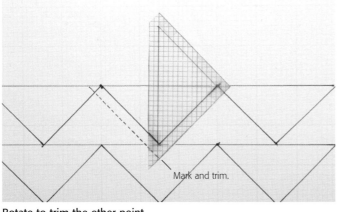

Rotate to trim the other point.

4. Now you can rely on the template's cropped edges to cut out patches primed for proficient piecing.

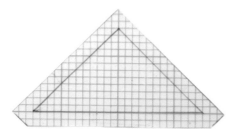

Consider these grooming techniques cardinal procedure. Neat and tidy templates with evenly matched edges are crucial for accurate piecing alignment. Don't even think about trimming a template without coordinating it to its neighbor—you risk shortchanging the amount of seam allowance needed. Chances are you will use common sense and clip it at a sensible angle, while the required slant is actually more eccentric and impossible to predict.

Align every template to either its adjoining template or the diagram, right sides together, sewing line to sewing line, and trim away any plastic peeping past its partner. You'll shed excess seam allowance and waste less fabric. Also, by arranging patches cut edge to cut edge, you'll eliminate the need for pinning before stitching.

Bending the Template

We've already talked about finding different backgrounds that visually blend and camouflage the seams. Another option is to fill adjacent patches with the same fabric in such a way that the audience perceives the single fabric to be continuous from patch to patch. I used this option in Block 5D (page 79). Even though the motifs bend and turn a corner, they don't seem to be interrupted by a seam. To pull this off, I must make the pattern of fabric in Patch 1 resume at exactly the point where it ended in Patch 2.

Now that we understand the setup, we can formulate the question: How do you get that specific portion of motif to wiggle its way into the template?

Once again, see-through template plastic is our enabler. The key to this construction strategy is to align the templates in an unusual way: overlap the bottom seam allowance of Template G1 onto the top seam allowance of Template H2 and then overlap the bottom seam allowance of Template H2 onto the top seam allowance of Template I3, so the sewing lines sit on top of each other. To set the stage, I positioned this band of templates on the fabric, seamline on top of seamline. I traced hints onto each template, taking care to copy lots of hints in the seam allowance and along the seams, where matching is essential. I like to copy enough hints to make identifying repeats a cinch.

This template technique ensures accurate patch alignment because it takes into account the all-important seam allowance, so you don't have to think about it. What have we learned from this? Templates made from see-through material are good.

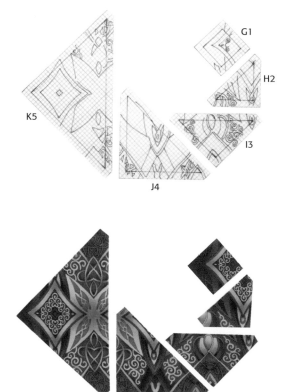

Bending the template

A Cut Too Small

This afternoon, I picked up the wrong template and cut out eight identical but slightly too-small patches. I didn't realize the error until I attempted to piece it to the next patch. This prima donna fabric is one of those huge repeats, so cutting another eight wasn't an option. I fixed the mistake by making a template the correct size without a seam allowance. After centering the new template on the old one, I traced the motif's original hints onto the new template. Then I placed this new template on the wrong side of each of the eight patches and lightly drew around the edges, marking the correct sewing line. Next, I marked the sewing line on the patches that my boo-boos were going to be sewn to. The seam allowance is a little smaller on the "mistake" patches now, but I can still align this patch precisely with its neighbor, right sides together, by pinning the marked sewing lines to each other.

No matter how inventive our quiltmaking notions get, the classic piecing hierarchy still rules. Construction always begins by piecing single patches together to create the smallest units. Small units combine to form larger units, which in turn join to make horizontal, vertical, or diagonal rows. The rows are joined sequentially until the puzzle block is complete. The mechanics of piecing give birth to the designs you concocted in the templating phase. The whole is always greater than the sum of its parts.

Your Sewing Machine

Any sewing machine that makes an even straight stitch is appropriate. Set the stitch length at 10 to 12 stitches per inch. Determine how you will sew an accurate ¼″ seam allowance on your machine. On some machines, the edge of the presser foot is exactly ¼″ from the needle. Other machines come with a magnetic or screw-on accessory to indicate sewing lines. If your machine has no markings at all, make your own. Stick a piece of masking tape on the throat plate. Measure from the needle ¼″ to the right, using the same ruler or graph paper grid you used to draft the design, and mark a line on the tape with your fine-point pen. When you sew, keep the edge of the patches lined up with this marking.

Sewing the Blocks

Each block in the Workbook (pages 51–91) has its own piecing sequence. When you work on blocks of your own design, first sew the mirror image and prima donna units together. These patches provide the all-important visual flow; give them your undivided attention so that they come together flawlessly.

Prima Donna Units

Begin by placing the patches right sides together so that the cut edges and corners that will be joined line up exactly. (Now do you see why we trimmed off the dog-ears so precisely?) Sew the pieces together, from edge to edge, using a ¼″ seam allowance.

To save time, sew identical units all at once. After sewing the first seam, don't remove the pieces from the machine and don't lift the presser foot. Just layer another set of patches and continue sewing, assembly-line style, until you've completed them all. You'll end up with what looks like a string of sausages that can be snipped apart into individual units. Open the units and check the matches at the seams. Hope that they are perfect. Lately, I've been backtacking at the beginning and end of each unit's seamline to make the stitching more secure during the subsequent pressing and handling. The only time I bemoan this instinct is when I have to rip a boo-boo later.

After you sew a seam, press it. You can press seams open or toward the darker fabric. Spritz a little water from a spray bottle onto a bulky seam to press it into submission.

As the block assembly progresses, you'll be joining units to other patches or units to units. To sew a long seam, begin by matching and pinning the ends. Next, match and pin the corresponding joints, from the center out, easing in the excess fabric. Place pins approximately 2″ apart. In a unit composed of patches with points, an X shape is created where four seams intersect. To sew a precise point, the needle must travel through the intersection of the X when the two units are joined.

Tip To control bias distortion when sewing an on-grain edge to an off-grain edge, layer the patches so the on-grain edge is on the bottom.

Holiday Puzzle Quilt, 2004, 50″ × 66″, designed and machine pieced by Paula Nadelstern, machine quilted by Jackie Kunkel. See the quilt diagram with block placement on page 50.

Strip Piecing/Power Stitching

I have to cut and sew prima donna patches one by one. But I've discovered a shortcut, based on strip piecing, for adding itty-bitty, odd-shaped allover patches. Because an allover pattern looks exactly the same from any angle, I don't need to worry about how the template falls. Long story short: Sew a strip of allover fabric to its neighboring fussy-cut patch, make one template incorporating both patches, and cut out both simultaneously. The result is a two-patch unit, complete with seam allowance, that looks like it was born that way.

Prima donna fabric (1) + allover fabric (2)

EXAMPLE 1

I want the intricate motif selected for Patch 1 to float on the background. To create this effect, I based my fabric choice for Patch 2 on the background color of the prima donna fabric used for Patch 1 (see Seemingly Seamless, page 15).

1. Trace the motif for Patch 1 onto Template 1 and use it to cut out Patch 1 (see page 39).

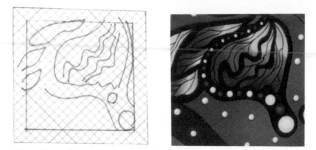

Trace Template 1 and cut out patch.

2. Make a template that encompasses patches 1 and 2. Add a ¼″ seam allowance all around and cut out. Using a ruler, extend the seamline into the seam allowance at each end to ensure accurate placement along the full length of the sewing line. Align Template 1 + 2 on Template 1 and transfer the hints.

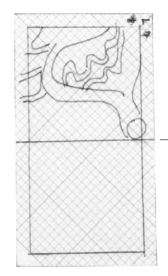

Extend seamline into seam allowance.

Create Template 1 + 2.

3. Rotary cut strips of Fabric 2. The strip(s) must be long enough to accommodate the total number of patches needed (see Calculating the Strip Width, page 47).

4. Place Patch 1 on the Fabric 2 strip, right sides together. Make sure the patch is placed in the correct orientation. Machine stitch. Repeat, sewing all the units at the same time, assembly-line style. Remember to reverse half of the units.

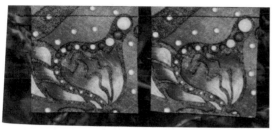

Sew the patches to the strip.

5. Press the seam allowance toward the darker patch. Position Template 1 + 2 on a stripped-together unit. Match the hints drawn on the template to the corresponding motifs in Patch 1. Align the sewing line marked on the template with the seam made in step 4. Hold the template firmly in place and trace around it to mark a visible, precise line on the Fabric 2 strip.

Align Template 1 + 2 to the motifs in Patch 1.

6. Cut out Patch 1 + 2, using either scissors or a small rotary cutter, aiming down the middle of the marked line.

7. Repeat step 6 until you have enough accurately pieced units, each complete with seam allowance and ready for its next assignment. Doesn't it look as if the patches were meticulously cut and pieced together?

CALCULATING THE STRIP WIDTH

You'll need the two-patch template and a transparent ruler. Place ¼″ of the ruler on one side of the sewing line (representing the seam allowance), while the rest of the ruler lies on the portion of the template that represents the piece that will be added. Read the ruler measurement at the widest part of the template. In this example, you need to cut a 2⅝″-wide strip for the pieced-on patch.

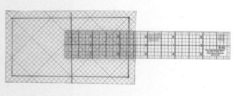

EXAMPLE 2

Here's a slightly different scenario. In this case, both Patch 1 and Patch 2 will be filled with allovers. Because no prima donna fabric is involved, neither patch needs its own template.

Two overall fabrics

1. Make Template 1 + 2, add a ¼″ seam allowance, and cut out. Extend the seamline into the seam allowance.

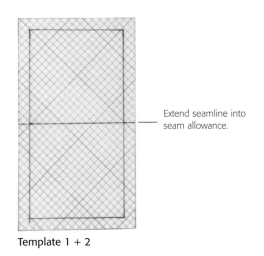

Extend seamline into seam allowance.

Template 1 + 2

2. Rotary cut strips of both fabrics.

3. Sew the 2 strips together. Press the seam allowance toward the darker fabric.

4. Position Template 1 + 2 on top, aligning the sewing line marked on the template with the seam made in step 3. Trace around the edge of the template. Repeat to mark the appropriate number of 1 + 2 L(eft) patches. If using mirror image patches, flip over the template to mark the same number of 1 + 2 R(ight) patches. Cut out.

Here are some more power stitching pointers:

■ Press after every piecing sequence. Press seams open when possible; otherwise, press toward the darker patch. Spritz the fabric with water from a spray bottle and press seams into submission.

■ Prune your strip-pieced units. Check out the wrong side. Does the seam allowance extend beyond the necessary ¼″? Use common sense and trim off the excess tidbits to foster a less bulky seam.

■ Take the opportunity to trim the patches. We try our best, but between sewing and pressing and handling, stuff stretches (or somehow shrinks). Every new template made to guide a strip-piecing procedure is an opportunity to correct the piece in progress and pull it back in line. Align the template to the patchwork, line up the seams, and trim off any fabric sticking out beyond the template. I trim a lot, often using the handy-dandy Brooklyn Revolver (a circular rotary mat mounted on a lazy Susan) and a small rotary cutter.

Setting the Blocks

The arrangement of a group of blocks in the quilt top is called the layout or set. Arrange, rearrange, shift, shuffle—nothing is better than working on a design wall that allows you to step back for a true perspective. I know: I worked on a 30″-round kitchen table in a two-bedroom apartment for more than twenty years without this option. (If you are wondering "How did she do it?" please know that after two years in my own design wall–enhanced studio, I wonder the same thing.)

The three quilts shown in this book use the identical twelve-block set, divided into four horizontal rows and three vertical rows. A large bedspread might be a whopping 42 blocks, set six across and seven down. Juggle the 12″-square patchwork blocks offered in the Workbook (pages 51–91) into your own well-balanced act. Or pick completely different quilt blocks from the ones in this book and experiment until you've discovered two variations that convey unique visual effects. Repeat a favorite square multiple times. Alternate two different ones in a checkerboard. Turn them all on-point.

Once you determine how many blocks will fit horizontally and vertically, draw your quilt design to scale on graph paper. Let one graph paper square equal one square inch of the quilt top. Include sashing strips and cornerstones between the blocks, if you wish. You can use this line drawing to calculate yardage and determine a piecing sequence. Remember, however, that it is a plan of the finished quilt's dimensions and does not include the ¼″ seam allowance that must be added to every edge.

Here are the cutting and sewing directions to make the quilt settings shown on pages 7, 34, and 45.

 A design wall is a flat, vertical surface that lets you view and evaluate your quilt-blocks-in-progress. To convert an available wall into a design wall, simply line it with batting or plain flannel fabric to hold patches in place without pinning.

YARDAGE

Block frames: 1 yard
Sashing: 1¼ yards
Cornerstones: ¼ yard
Backing: 3 yards
Batting: 54″ × 70″

CUTTING

Block frames: Cut 24 strips 1½″ × 12½″.
Cut 24 strips 1½″ × 14½″.
Sashing: Cut 31 strips 2½″ × 14½″.
Cornerstones: Cut 20 squares 2½″ × 2½″.

ASSEMBLY

1. Sew the side frames to the block. Press toward the frame. Then sew the top and bottom frames to the block. Press toward the frame.

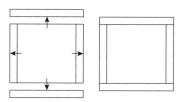

2. Sew the blocks and sashing strips together into rows. Press toward the sashing.

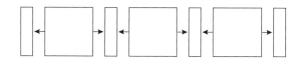

3. Sew the cornerstones and remaining sashing strips into rows. Press toward the sashing.

4. Sew the rows together. Press.

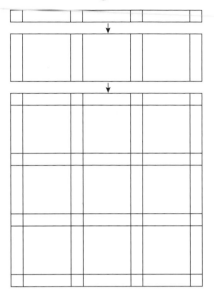

Quilt Diagrams

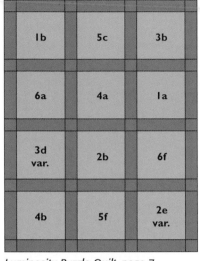

Luminosity Puzzle Quilt, page 7

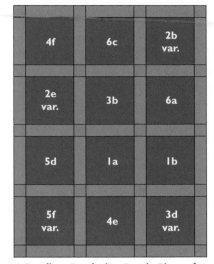

A Puzzling, Perplexing Purple Piece of Patchwork to Ponder, page 34

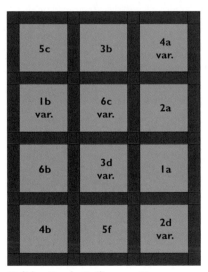

Holiday Puzzle Quilt, page 45

Nothing takes the juice out of the creative process

more than trying to parse the experience after the fact. But now that everything's all sewn up, I have a unique chance to tell you about the blocks that bombed and about those that were the successes. Be my guest. Analyze, evaluate, scrutinize, dissect. Critique the blocks on the following pages and ask yourself, "Why? How? Why do I like this but not that? How did this happen, and what did that?"

So many blocks, so many questions. Close your eyes and when you pop them open, identify the primary focal point. What caused it? Which route does your eye want to take? If you feel a rhythm, how would you describe it? Is there a dimensional quality? What about a light from within? Decipher the figure-and-ground relationships. Hunt for seams. When something catches your eye, explore the element that hooked it.

The Puzzle Block Workbook contains six block designs, each with six different variations. Piecing diagrams (so you can avoid sewing into a corner) are on pages 90–91. Block templates A through K are on pages 92–93. Blank block diagrams to photocopy are on page 94.

"when something catches your eye, explore the element that hooked it."

BLOCK 1A

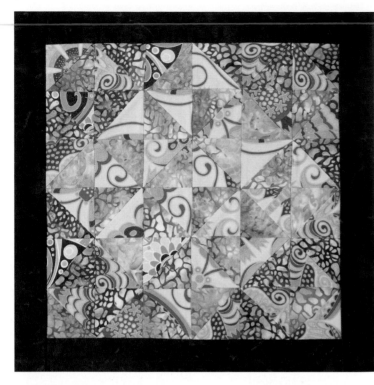

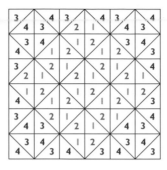

Although Fabric 1 qualifies for symmetrical status, I treated it like an allover. Without a fussy cut to worry about, I needed only one template. The design plan called for sorting both fabrics into their respective sections of dark and light. I wanted patches A1 and A2 to produce a focal point—the inner diamond—and patches A3 and A4 to form a receding frame. This meant cutting out lots of potential patches, placing them on a design wall, and stepping back for a reaction. Only in context could each patch's relative lightness or darkness be perceived.

TEMPLATE	PATCH	PROCESS	FABRIC
A	1	Cut 18	1 (light)
A	1 + 2	Make 18	1 + 2 (light)
A	3	Cut 18	1 (dark)
A	3 + 4	Make 18	1 + 2 (dark)

A1, A3

A1 + A2
A3 + A4

1 + 2

3 + 4

BLOCK 1B

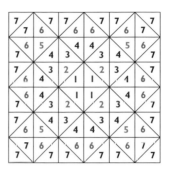

This ornate, regally colored star brims with elaborate detail and interlaced patterns. Fabric 1 provided five different motifs. This time I opted for elements that appear similar to one another rather than milking every ounce of variety from a single fabric. The repetition of identical motifs causes the eye to move from element to repeated element. A profusion of analogous motifs expands the field of search, compelling the eye to keep moving, encouraging a dynamic sensation. Fabric 3, a crackling magenta batik, adds shading and extra color. It also blurs some interior edges, making the outcome more interesting by pulling it out of predictable focus.

TEMPLATE	PATCH	PROCESS	FABRIC
A	1	Cut 2 L and 2 R	1
A	2	Cut 4	1
A	3	Cut 4 L and 4 R	1
A	3 + 4	Make 4 L and 4 R	1 + 3
A	5	Cut 4	1
A	4 + 5	Make 4	1 + 3
A	6	Cut 8 L and 8 R	1
A	6 + 7	Make 8 L and 8 R	1 + 2
A	7 + 7	Make 4	2 + 2

A1

A2

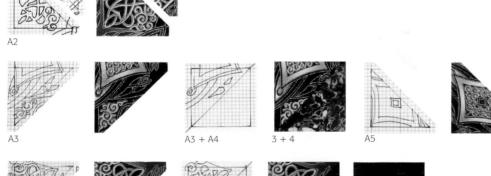

A3   A3 + A4   3 + 4   A5   A5 + A4   5 + 4

A6   A6 + A7   6 + 7   7 + 7

BLOCK 1C

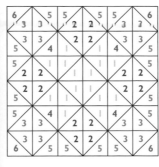

Of the 30-odd blocks made for this book, this design was the hardest to resolve. When my original choice for Fabric 1 bombed, a long auditioning spell ensued because I stubbornly refused to ditch fabrics 2 and 3. I believed the little cream-colored motifs in Fabric 2 would function like sea foam, simultaneously energizing and lightening, and I loved Fabric 3's graded stripes and silky sheen (I "cottonized" this silk fabric with fusible interfacing).

Although Fabric 1 forms a central star, it does not become the focal point. In some places, the star's edges, instead of being clearly defined, dissolve into incomplete contours. An ambiguous relationship is set up with the silk stripe, which ends up functioning as the background.

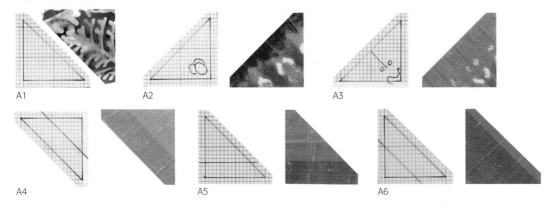

A1 A2 A3

A4 A5 A6

TEMPLATE	PATCH	PROCESS	FABRIC
A	1	Cut 16	1
A	2	Cut 16	2
A	3	Cut 16	2
A	4	Cut 4	3
A	5	Cut 8 L and 8 R	3
A	6	Cut 4	3

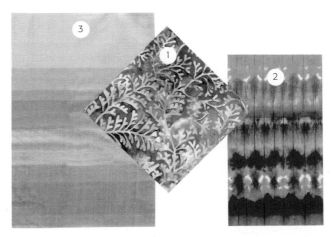

BLOCK 1D

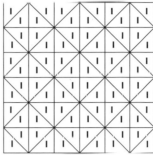

These dancing stars owe their twinkling transience to the irregularity of the rays in the celestial print. Since portraying an illusion of motion was my goal, I deliberately chose rays of varying lengths. In this combination, they appear to flicker; the viewer half expects them to change at any moment.

The single template is marked with a fragment of the sun's inner circle and a sample ray to suggest direction, not necessarily to duplicate precisely. When I placed the template on the fabric, I caught a single ray and the black background, taking care not to allow any residual motifs into the window area of the patch. (I used a black permanent marker to color over the few that tagged along.) It's important to cut half of the patches facing left and half facing right, not 72 in the same direction. Sew together a left and right triangle to form a square.

TEMPLATE	PATCH	PROCESS	FABRIC
A	1	Cut 36 L and 36 R	1

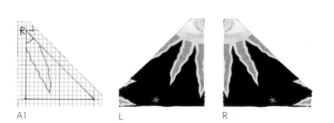

Partial rays along the patch edges disappear into the seam allowance.

BLOCK 1E

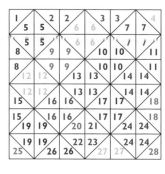

I positioned the same template as many different ways as possible on this color-filled, skinny-striped fabric, cutting four identical patches each time. Using a design wall, I played with the resulting squares on point, fitting them together while aiming to eke out every smidgen of visual disparity. Just to be ornery, I built one square from four dissimilar patches. Can you find it?

TEMPLATE	PROCESS	FABRIC
A	Cut 13 sets of 4	1
A	Cut 8 sets of 2	1
A	Cut 4 sets of 1	1

BLOCK 1F

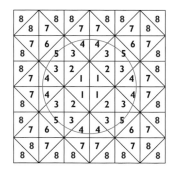

The fabric made me do it. In one of my recent classes, the purple pears peeked out from a student's stash, and I was on it in a New York minute, offering to trade my goods for hers. The fabric's curvaceous shapes, solid black ground, and gold accents challenged me to build a circle.

I used a compass to draft a true circle on a life-size diagram of the block. I then traced sections of the circular line onto the appropriate templates (A3, A4, and A5) and found comparable curvatures among the fruits, positioning the template so the portion intended to be a circle lay on the color purple and the rest fell on empty black ground.

TEMPLATE	PATCH	PROCESS	FABRIC
A	1	Cut 4	1
A	2	Cut 4	1
A	3	Cut 4 L and 4 R	1
A	4	Cut 4 L and 4 R	1
A	5	Cut 4	1
A	5 + 6	Make 4	1 + 4
A	7	Cut 8 L and 8 R	2
A	7 + 8	Make 8 L and 8 R	2 + 3
A	8 + 8	Make 4	3 + 3

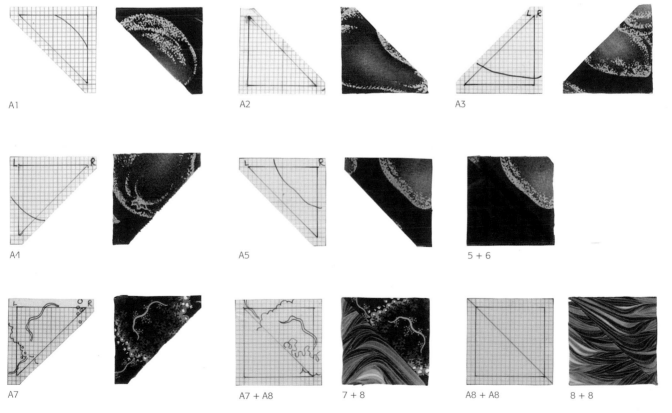

I fussy cut Patch A7 and strip pieced it to Fabric 3, which is an allover.
Then I cut Patch A7 + A8 with a combination template. I used the
same procedure to produce the A5 + A6 patches and the four corner
patches, A8 + A8.

BLOCK 2A

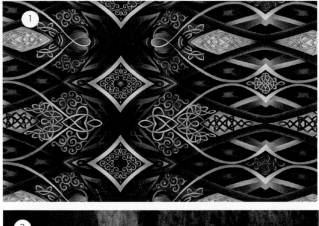

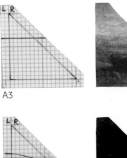

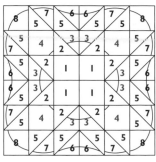

The center star achieves superstar status when lit from behind by a glowing circle of a mildly discordant yellow. I created this halo effect using broad bands of color in a rainbow-hued cloth (Fabric 2). First, on a full-size diagram, I sketched a path for the fabric to follow. I placed templates on the diagram and traced the path from the diagram onto the see-through templates. Next, I placed the templates on Fabric 2 so the traced line sat where two color bands met. Patches 3 and 4 are yellow and reddish-pink. Successive colors of the rainbow filled Patch 5 first and then patches 6, 7, and 8.

TEMPLATE	PATCH	PROCESS	FABRIC
B	1	Cut 2 L and 2 R	1
A	2	Cut 4 L and 4 R	1
A	3	Cut 4 L and 4 R	2
B	4	Cut 4	2
A	5	Cut 8 L and 8 R	2
A	6	Cut 4 L and 4 R	2
A	7	Cut 4 L and 4 R	2
B	8	Cut 4	2

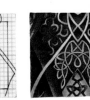

B1

B4

A3

A2

A5

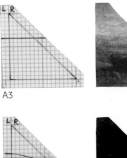

A6

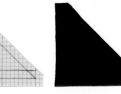

A7

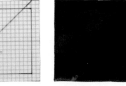

B8

BLOCK 2B

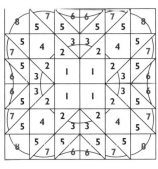

Block 2A (page 58) suggested a what-if idea: What if I pieced the same center star to neighboring fabrics that were very dark instead of yellow and reddish-pink? When the color that functions as the ground in Patch 2 connects to a similar color in Patch 3, would the seamline between them be disguised? Would the graceful, curvy, mushroom-toned lines in Patch 2 appear to pop and float on the fabric?

Well, what do you think? Was it a thought worth pursuing?

Fabric 3 is a symbiotic fabric. It doesn't look like much in a single patch, but it ably illustrates how a patchwork whole is greater than the sum of its parts. Putting the Fabric 2's contrasting colors near the outer edges makes it easier to see the pathways intended for Patches 6, 7, and 8.

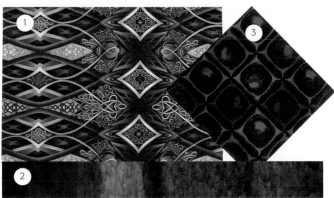

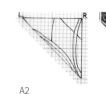

TEMPLATE	PATCH	PROCESS	FABRIC
B	1	Cut 2 L and 2 R	1
A	2	Cut 4 L and 4 R	1
A	3	Cut 4 L and 4 R	2
B	4	Cut 4	2
A	5	Cut 8 L and 8 R	3
A	6	Cut 4 L and 4 R	2
A	7	Cut 4 L and 4 R	2
B	8	Cut 4	2

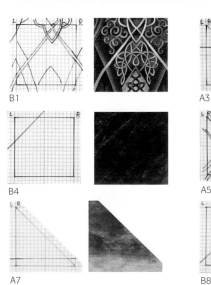

B1

A3

A2

B4

A5

A6

A7

B8

BLOCK 2C

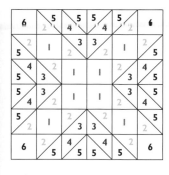

In this shadowy concoction of low-contrast fabrics, all of the fabrics' backgrounds merge and reemerge as negative space while eye-catching jewel-tone accents leap forward and float like stained glass. Only when you move up close and personal do the patchwork shapes and seams become apparent.

Fabric 1 is a computer-generated textile print. On Template A2, I marked where I wanted to catch the fabric's iridescent green curve. The viewer's eye can't help but follow the pathway created by this recurring motif as it travels around the block, searching for secondary focal points and accents to illuminate.

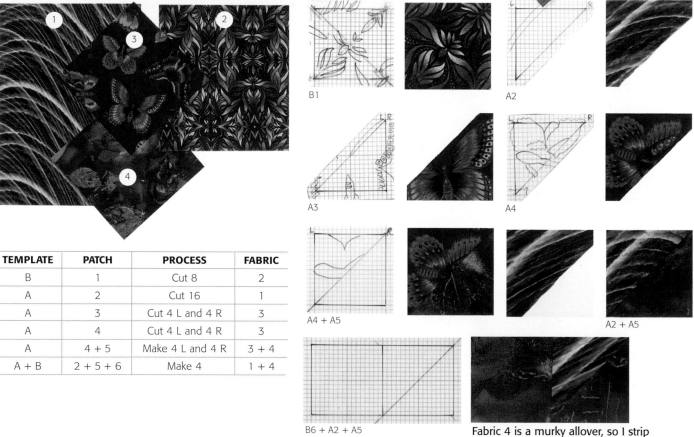

TEMPLATE	PATCH	PROCESS	FABRIC
B	1	Cut 8	2
A	2	Cut 16	1
A	3	Cut 4 L and 4 R	3
A	4	Cut 4 L and 4 R	3
A	4 + 5	Make 4 L and 4 R	3 + 4
A + B	2 + 5 + 6	Make 4	1 + 4

B1

A2

A3

A4

A4 + A5

A2 + A5

B6 + A2 + A5

Fabric 4 is a murky allover, so I strip pieced it to Patch A2 rather than cutting out individual pieces.

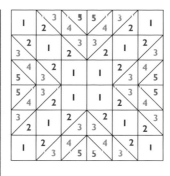

BLOCK 2D

See-through templates facilitated my looking at these fabrics in new, unanticipated ways. Do you like how the big black circles in Fabric 2 disappear? I like the repetition of twinkling "corners" of dots proffered by the tree fabric. Placing the template on slightly different portions of dots creates a more animated effect, less static than the exact same amount each time.

TEMPLATE	PATCH	PROCESS	FABRIC
B	1	Cut 12	2
A	2	Cut 16	4
A	3	Cut 16	3
A	4	Cut 8	3
A	5	Cut 4 L and 4 R	1

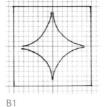

B1

A2

A3

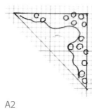

A4

A5

BLOCK 2E

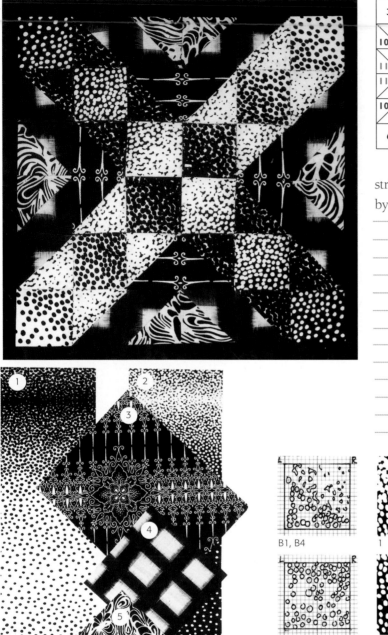

A visual conundrum results when two fabrics that are black-and-white opposites attract the eye and tempt it to figure out what went where and what's doing what. Instead of a formal balance, the initial emphasis on the brighter diagonal stripe strikes an appealing asymmetrical pose surrounded by symmetrical repetition.

TEMPLATE	PATCH	PROCESS	FABRIC
B	1	Cut 2	2
B	2	Cut 2	2
B	3	Cut 2	2
B	4	Cut 2	1
B	5	Cut 2	1
B	6	Cut 2	1
A	7	Cut 8	1
A	8	Cut 8	2
A	9	Cut 4 L and 4 R	3
A	10	Cut 16	4
A	11	Cut 8	5

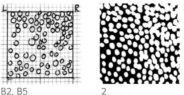

B1, B4   1   4

B2, B5   2   5

B3, B6   3   6

A7, A8   7   8   A9   9   A10   10   11

BLOCK 2F

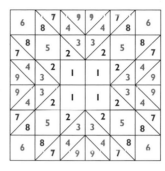

The question is, what happens when the usual relationship between figure and ground is reversed? What if the center star becomes negative space surrounded by fabulous ornate motifs? I love this answer.

TEMPLATE	PATCH	PROCESS	FABRIC
B	1	Cut 4	5
A	2	Cut 8	5
A	3	Cut 4 L and 4 R	3
A	4	Cut 4 L and 4 R	3
B	5	Cut 4	3
B	6	Cut 4	3
A	7	Cut 4 L and 4 R	4
A	8	Cut 4 L and 4 R	2
A	9	Cut 4 L and 4 R	1

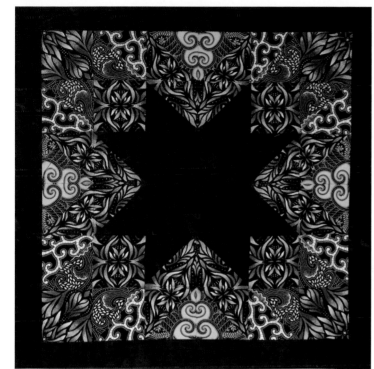

A3

A4

B5

B6

A8

A7

A9

BLOCK 3A

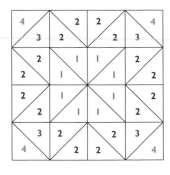

Because all three fabrics are bilaterally symmetrical (yes, even the two "marbleized" fabrics function like the wings of a butterfly), they provide mirror image patches. But note how Template C1 is not centered along the "belly" of the butterfly. Instead, it is cut off-grain, creating an irregular center motif. Template C2 is cut in a similar way, while templates C3 and C4 are symmetrical and centered.

TEMPLATE	PATCH	PROCESS	FABRIC
C	1	Cut 4 L and 4 R	2
C	2	Cut 8 L and 8 R	1
C	3	Cut 4	1
C	4	Cut 4	3

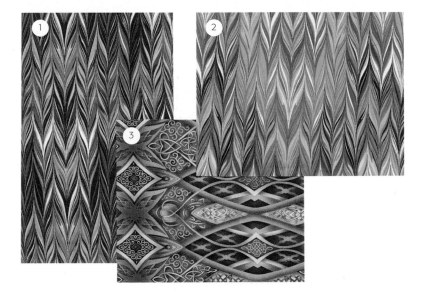

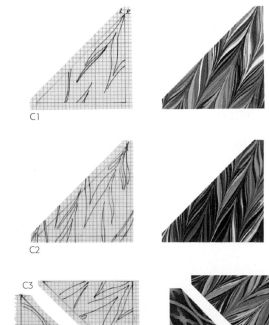

C1

C2

C3

C4

BLOCK 3B

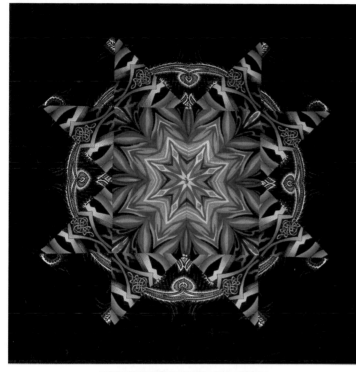

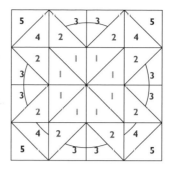

This block functions like a radial design because all the elements develop symmetrically around a common central point. To make the star, I placed Template C1 on the fabric off-grain rather than centered down the middle of a symmetrical motif. Template C2 is centered and symmetrical.

To enhance the circular illusion, I used a compass to draw a perfect circle in the full-size graph paper diagram. I erased parts of the line, so that the circle was visible only in selected patches, as if hiding behind the star. I traced these lines onto templates C3 and C4 and used the templates to search for motifs with equivalent curves. Fabric 1 provided the curves for both templates; in fact, it would be difficult to depict this circle, interrupted or not, with two different fabrics. Note the extra motifs that slipped into patch 3, creating secondary designs "inside" the circle.

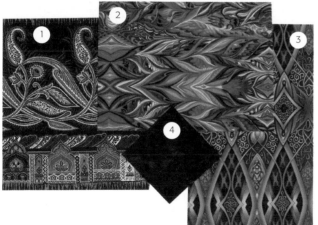

TEMPLATE	PATCH	PROCESS	FABRIC
C	1	Cut 4 L and 4 R	2
C	2	Cut 4 L and 4 R	3
C	3	Cut 4 L and 4 R	1
C	4	Cut 4	3
C	4 + 5	Make 4	4

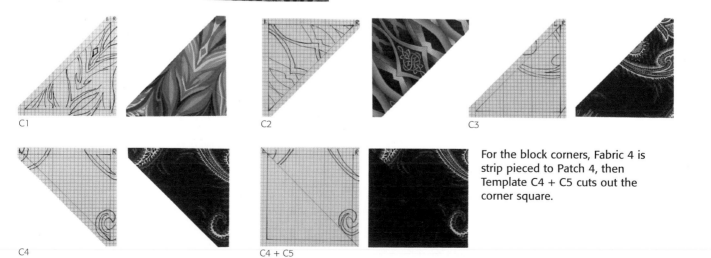

C1

C2

C3

C4

C4 + C5

For the block corners, Fabric 4 is strip pieced to Patch 4, then Template C4 + C5 cuts out the corner square.

BLOCK 3C

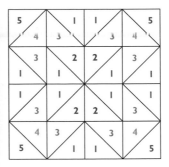

For this block, a single exuberant, symmetrical fabric is cut five different ways. Note that Patch 1 joins to Patch 2 and Patch 3 in a reverse direction.

TEMPLATE	PATCH	PROCESS	FABRIC
C	1	Cut 6 L and 6 R	1
C	2	Cut 2 L and 2 R	1
C	3	Cut 4 L and 4 R	1
C	4	Cut 4	1
C	5	Cut 4	1

C1   C2

C3

C4

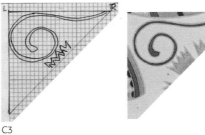

C5

BLOCK 3D

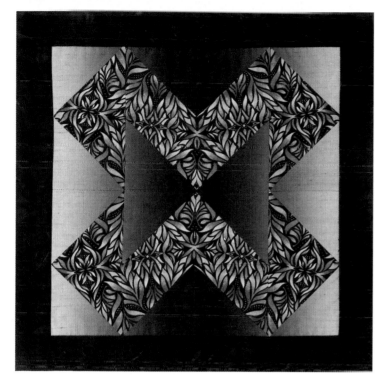

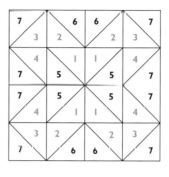

The "expected" luminous effect is to focus the light at the center of the block and shade the colors darker toward the periphery. In this block, I placed the anticipated glow on the outside edges, for a gentle, undulating rhythm. To create this unusual tonal background, I interfaced Fabric 1, a kimono silk purchased on sale in Japan, and used three different portions.

Meanwhile, Fabric 2 maneuvers itself out from the center as if it were one continuous piece of fabric instead of four patched-together triangles. The resulting form looks sculpted.

TEMPLATE	PATCH	PROCESS	FABRIC
C	1	Cut 2 L and 2 R	2
C	2	Cut 2 L and 2 R	2
C	3	Cut 2 L and 2 R	2
C	4	Cut 2 L and 2 R	2
C	5	Cut 2 L and 2 R	1
C	6	Cut 2 L and 2 R	1
C	7	Cut 4 L and 4 R	1

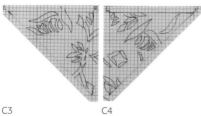

Use Template C5 to cut patches 5, 6, and 7.

BLOCK 3E

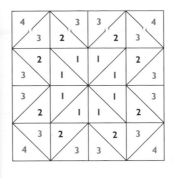

Both fabrics function as stripes. Note the marked line on Template C1. By placing it along the line of color contrast where light olive meets rust at the top of Fabric 1, I created a slim wedge of eye-catching olive in Patch 1. I aimed for a narrow splash of olive, knowing it would meet itself and multiply at the center of the block.

To cut Patch 2, I used Fabric 1 again in a similar way with Template C2. This time, a bright orangy-rust stripe is adjacent to a mass of dark burgundy. When the brighter color visually attaches itself to the corners of Patch 1, it blurs the straight seams between Patches 1 and 2 and suggests a slight curve.

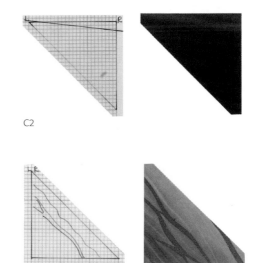

TEMPLATE	PATCH	PROCESS	FABRIC
C	1	Cut 4 L and 4 R	1
C	2	Cut 4 L and 4 R	1
C	3	Cut 6 L and 6 R	2
C	4	Cut 4	2

C1

C2

C3

C4

BLOCK 3F

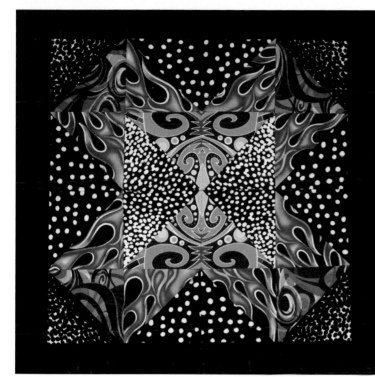

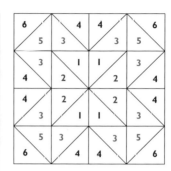

Fabrics 1 and 2 are intentional opposites. Fabric 1 is filled with black dots on a white ground, while Fabric 2's black ground overflows with white spots. In both cases, the splatter travels from sparse to dense. Template C2 catches this shift in Fabric 2.

Who would have thought the happy butterflies in reliably mirror imaged Fabric 3 would seamlessly connect to Fabric 5's dancing flames, a print that looks like it was born to be biker wear? Thanks to the black backgrounds, the seams between patches C3 and C4 disappear and the boogying flames seem free and sinuous.

I love the grayed-down, indistinct influence of Fabric 6. I could have strip pieced it to Patch 6, but I opted to fussy cut it, grabbing a corner patch from Fabric 1 at its most densely spotted section. Once again, a black-and-white palette lives up to its reputation as an arbiter, capably finding common ground between strange patch fellows.

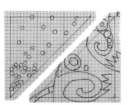
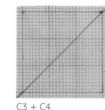
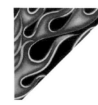

TEMPLATE	PATCH	PROCESS	FABRIC
C	1	Cut 2 L and 2 R	3
C	2	Cut 2 L and 2 R	2
C	3	Cut 4 L and 4 R	5
C	3 + 4	Make 4 L and 4 R	5 + 4
C	5	Cut 4	6
C	6	Cut 4	1

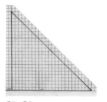

C2   C1

C3 + C4

3 + 4

C5, C6

Fabric 4, an allover, is strip pieced to Patch 3 using a C3 + C4 template. There is no need for a separate C4 template.

BLOCK 4A

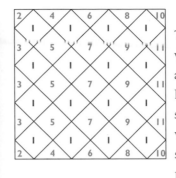

The only clue drawn on Template D1 is an egg shape, which is intended to align on any flower center in Fabric 1. Fabric 2 features an oversized, painterly stripe filled with lively, directional brush strokes. By cutting sets of patches from the same section of the design, I was able to organize and direct the traffic vertically through the block.

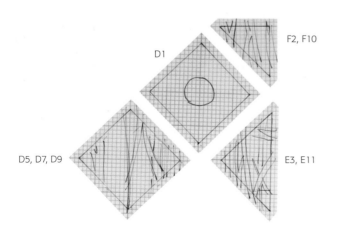

TEMPLATE	PATCH	PROCESS	FABRIC
D	1	Cut 16	1
F	2	Cut 2	2
E	3	Cut 3	2
E	4	Cut 2	2
D	5	Cut 3	2
E	6	Cut 2	2
D	7	Cut 3	2
E	8	Cut 2	2
D	9	Cut 3	2
F	10	Cut 2	2
E	11	Cut 3	2

D1

F2, F10

D5, D7, D9

E3, E11

Cutting sets of patches from a wacky stripe creates vertical movement through the block.

BLOCK 4B

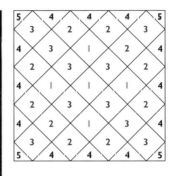

For this interlocking design to work, there had to be strong visual contrast between fabrics 2 and 3. Rendered with light and shadow, as well as strong, irregular curves, Fabric 1 proved to be a zinger, pulsing with visual movement.

I love to randomly dissect cloths like fabrics 1 and 4 and reinterpret them in patchwork. The result brims with a lively spontaneity. Although Fabric 4 has more colors than Fabric 1, portions of the two bleed into each other in an indistinguishable way. Together they form a common ground—pleasingly brighter toward the center—from which I could display the red and purple shibori-clad object. Using two fabrics creates more depth and a more interesting finished product.

TEMPLATE	PATCH	PROCESS	FABRIC
D	1	Cut 5	1
D	2	Cut 10	2
D	3	Cut 10	3
E	4	Cut 12	4
F	5	Cut 4	4

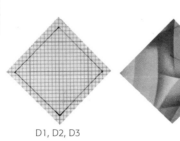

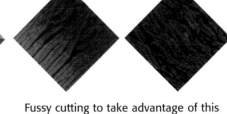

D1, D2, D3

E4

Fussy cutting to take advantage of this shibori-inspired stripe, made subtle by the ombré method of blending one color into another, leaves holes in fabrics 1 and 2.

F5

BLOCK 4C

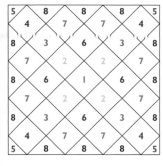

Long glowing spokes (each composed of four patches) start at the center and rapidly shoot out toward the corners. Eventually, the frenetic, high-contrast eruptions of white in Patch 6 draw attention back to the blue-green nucleus. The fact that each flare-up is slightly different increases the animation. If the bursts were identical, the result would be stilted.

TEMPLATE	PATCH	PROCESS	FABRIC
D	1	Cut 1	1
D	2	Cut 4	1
D	3	Cut 4	1
D	4	Cut 4	1
D + E	4 + 8	Make 4	1 + 3
F	5	Cut 4	1
D	6	Cut 4	1
D + E	7 + 8	Make 8	2 + 3

Allover fabrics 2 and 3 are stripped together and cut using the single D7 + E8 template. Use this same template to strip Fabric 3 to one side of each Patch 4.

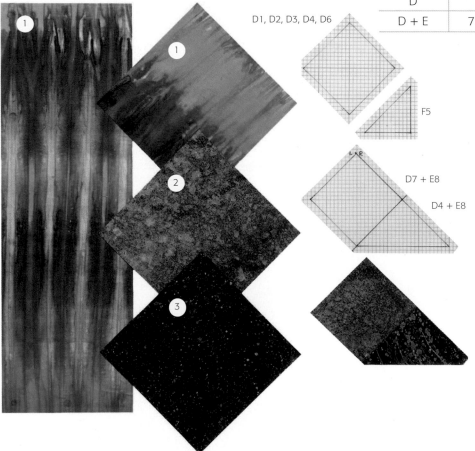

D1, D2, D3, D4, D6

F5

D7 + E8

D4 + E8

BLOCK 4D

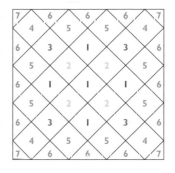

A solo fabric with even multihued stripes is exploited to the max and sliced into seven different templates. If you feel extra confident, use the same D template for all the square patches. But make sure to mark the cues in different colors, or in various combinations of dashed and dotted lines, so you don't confuse one patch with another.

TEMPLATE	PATCH	PROCESS	FABRIC
D	1	Cut 5	1
D	2	Cut 4	1
D	3	Cut 4	1
D	4	Cut 4	1
D	5	Cut 8	1
E	6	Cut 12	1
F	7	Cut 4	1

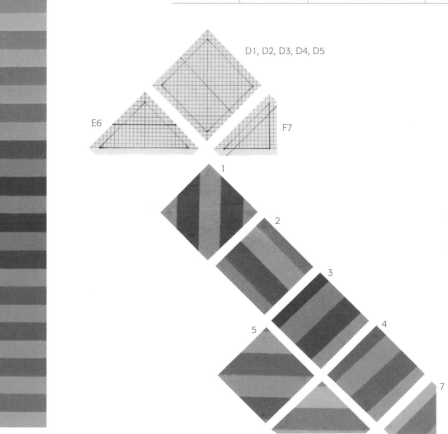

BLOCK 4E

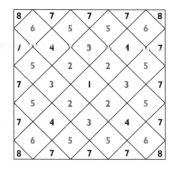

This dotty block rocks. The two fabrics are the same pattern; just the colorways differ. With the same black ground working double-time, it was easy to use them together effectively. Sometimes an artifact—a little unwanted doodad—tagged along with the chosen motif and had to be "erased" with a layer of permanent black marker.

TEMPLATE	PATCH	PROCESS	FABRIC
D	1	Cut 1	1
D	2	Cut 4	1
D	3	Cut 4	1
D	4	Cut 4	1
D	5	Cut 8	2
D	6	Cut 4	2
E	7	Cut 12	1
F	8	Cut 4	1

D1

D2

D3

D4

D5

D6

E7

F8

BLOCK 4F

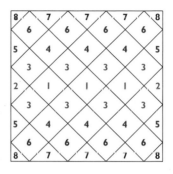

The repeat on life-size, lacy Fabric 1 is humongous. Luckily, I had yards and yards of this wonderful stuff, enough to construct a block (and fix a mistake) and establish a rhythm of recurring motifs that align gracefully from left to right. Stunning as this fabric is, the retro Victorian block needed something unexpected to catapult it beyond the ordinary. The hazy, surreal glow of Fabric 2 not only brightened the result but also introduced new motifs that reflect off one another in mysterious seamless connection.

TEMPLATE	PATCH	PROCESS	FABRIC
D	1	Cut 3	1
D	2*	Cut 2	1
D	3	Cut 8	2
D	4	Cut 6	1
D	5*	Cut 4	1
D	6	Cut 8	1
D + E	6 + 7	Make 6	1 + 3
D + F	6 + 8	Make 2	1 + 3
F	8	Cut 2	3

*Template D2 is half of Template D1 (plus seam allowance). Template D5 is half of Template D4 (plus seam allowance).

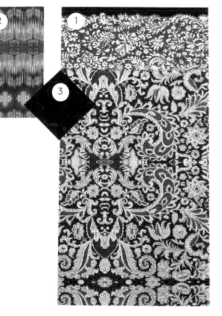

Patch 6, cut along one selvage, includes a lacy scallop and a bit of black ground. To continue the black ground, Fabric 3 is strip pieced to Patch 6 and then cut with combination templates.

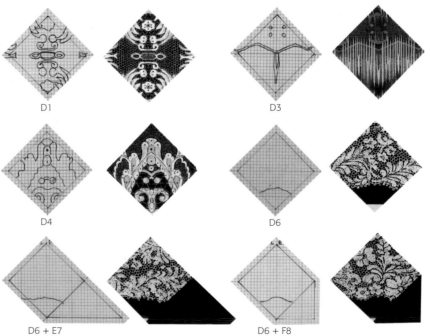

D1
D3
D4
D6
D6 + E7
D6 + F8

BLOCK 5A

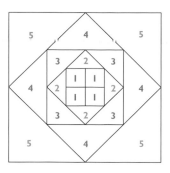

One striped fabric, five different patches. Because the objective was to reveal a wide range of diversity from a single fabric, I chose portions for each template that seemed dissimilar from each other rather than looking for commonality.

TEMPLATE	PATCH	PROCESS	FABRIC
G	1	Cut 4	1
H	2	Cut 4	1
I	3	Cut 4	1
J	4	Cut 4	1
K	5	Cut 4	1

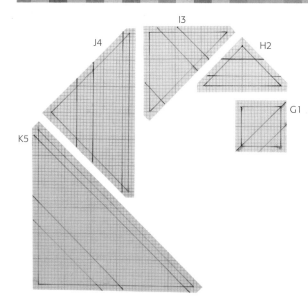

BLOCK 5B

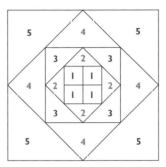

Once again, I used a single striped fabric. But this time, I used the same stripes multiple times to line up the patches, which resulted in a programmed diagonal path for the viewer's eye to travel.

TEMPLATE	PATCH	PROCESS	FABRIC
G	1	Cut 4	1
H	2	Cut 4	1
I	3	Cut 4	1
J	4	Cut 4	1
K	5	Cut 4	1

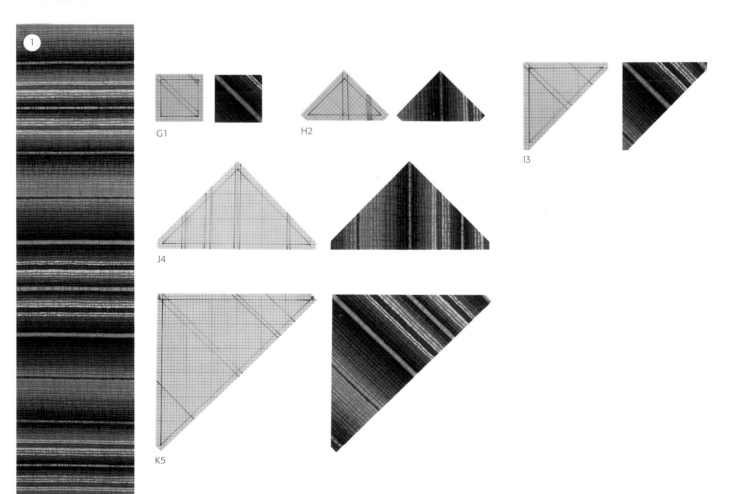

G1

H2

I3

J4

K5

BLOCK 5C

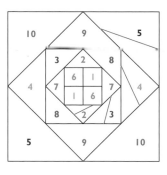

Another striped fabric, another plan. This muted rainbow of graded colors spans from selvage to selvage. I started by putting the darkest colors (the ones closest to the selvages) in the largest patches and then worked my way toward the center, getting progressively lighter. I fussy cut to obtain two shades in each triangular patch, using an angled line on the template to locate the color change on the fabric. The result is a soft, uninterrupted swirl of color and shading.

G1, G6

H2, H7

I3, I8

TEMPLATE	PATCH	PROCESS	FABRIC
G	1	Cut 2	1
H	2	Cut 2	1
I	3	Cut 2	1
J	4	Cut 2	1
K	5	Cut 2	1
G	6	Cut 2	1
H	7	Cut 2	1
I	8	Cut 2	1
J	9	Cut 2	1
K	10	Cut 2	1

J4, J9

K5, K10

BLOCK 5D

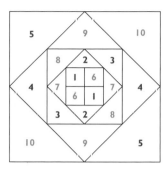

A complex prima donna and a fiery allover batik join forces in this powerful swirling design. The prima donna motifs flow from patch to patch, making the seams hard to detect (see Bending the Template, page 42). Fitting a prima donna together in this unrelenting manner is effective but exacting—and I'm not exact. The batik gave me the leeway I needed to true up the block. It also added that painterly luminescence I've grown to rely on.

TEMPLATE	PATCH	PROCESS	FABRIC
G	1	Cut 2	1
H	2	Cut 2	1
I	3	Cut 2	1
J	4	Cut 2	1
K	5	Cut 2	1
G	6	Cut 2	2
H	7	Cut 2	2
I	8	Cut 2	2
J	9	Cut 2	2
K	10	Cut 2	2

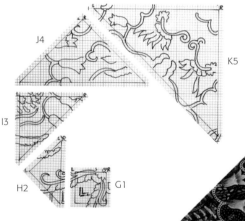

Use one set of templates to cut both fabrics. Disregard the marked hints on the templates when you cut the batik.

BLOCK 5E

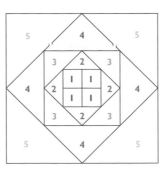

One arabesque-like fabric with a large repeat joins together into a magic carpet.

TEMPLATE	PATCH	PROCESS	FABRIC
G	1	Cut 2 L and 2 R	1
H	2	Cut 4	1
I	3	Cut 4	1
J	4	Cut 4	1
K	5	Cut 4	1

G1

H2

I3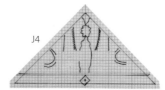

J4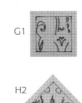

K5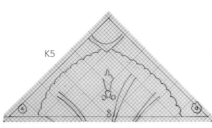

BLOCK 5F

A hodgepodge of prints unites in surprising harmony. Patch 5 is a good site for a pseudosymmetrical fabric. Even though these hand-drawn concentric circles are a little lopsided, the total impression imitates symmetry and provides closure in the corners. Fabric 3 is another noteworthy fabric. The ambiguity it creates softens the angular shapes.

TEMPLATE	PATCH	PROCESS	FABRIC
G	1	Cut 4	1
H	2	Cut 4	2
I	3	Cut 4	3
J	4	Cut 4	4
K	5	Cut 4	5

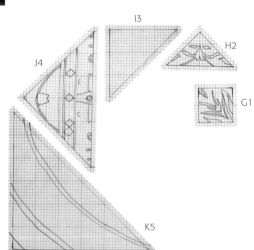

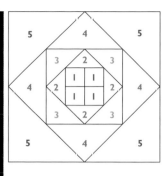

BLOCK 6A

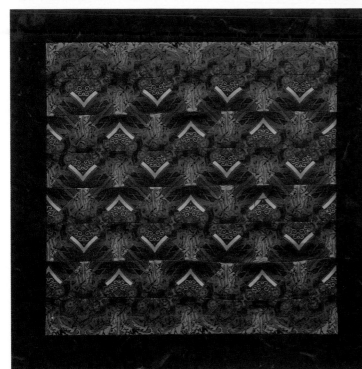

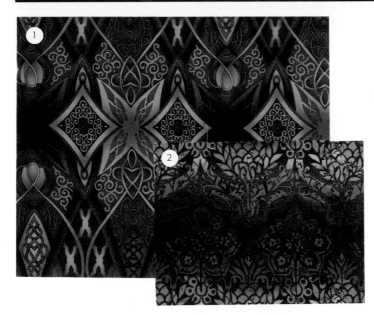

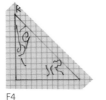

When Fabric 1 (a bilaterally symmetrical prima donna) joins with Fabric 2 (a pseudosymmetrical that is never called on to meet itself in a perfect match), it's hard to decipher the joints. The glowing, gold, dartlike motif marked on Template E1 flits around, cavorting with its clones while everything else recedes into the background.

TEMPLATE	PATCH	PROCESS	FABRIC
E	1	Cut 21	1
E	2	Cut 27	2
F	3	Cut 3L and 3R	1
F	4	Cut 5 L and 5 R	2
E	5	Cut 8	2

E1

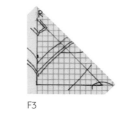

F3

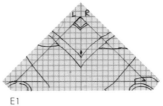

E2

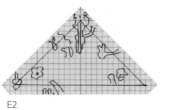

F4

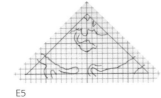

E5

BLOCK 6B

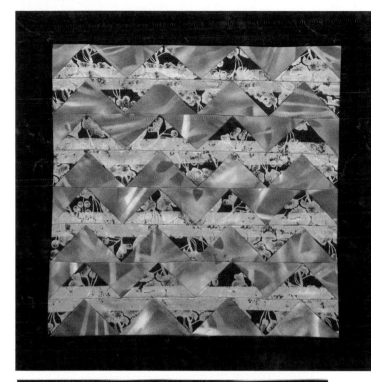

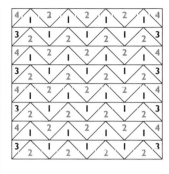

In Fabric 1, olive green squares sit against a mottled brown background. A layer of elegant gold ginkgo leaves are stamped on both. I marked a line on Template E1 to correspond to the demarcation between the olive square and the background. Every time I placed the template, I caught the same size strip of olive and a random amount of the gold ginkgos.

Fabric 2, an illuminating and active allover, is an old favorite. In this piecing scenario, it is strip pieced to Patch 1 and Patch 3 and cut out via templates E1 + E2, F4 + E1, and F3 + E2.

TEMPLATE	PATCH	PROCESS	FABRIC
E	1	Cut 28	1
E + E	1 + 2	Make 24	1 + 2
E + F	1 + 4	Make 4	1 + 2
F	3	Cut 4 L and 4 R	1
F + E	3 + 2	Make 4	1 + 2
F	4	Cut 4	2

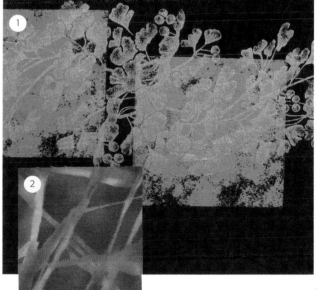

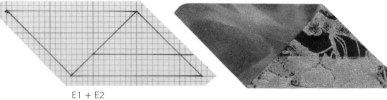

E1

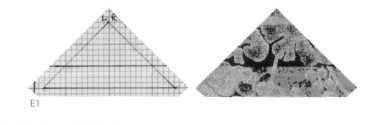

E1 + E2

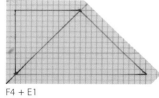

F4 + E1

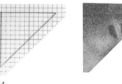

F4

BLOCK 6C

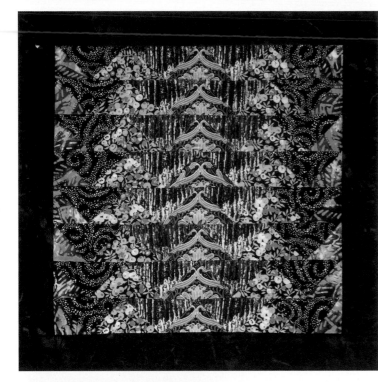

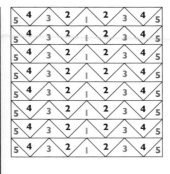

Our reliable standby, the black-and-white print, mediates between the formality of hundred-year-old patterns produced by Liberty of London (fabrics 1 and 5) and a contemporary batik (Fabric 3). Positioning the turquoise-and-black batik next to a black-background neighbor causes an interesting effect: The turquoise bits rise up while the ground recedes.

I have to fess up: Find Patch 1 in Row 4. See how the flowers have shrunk a wee bit? After auditioning multiple motifs from Fabric 1, I must have grabbed a reject when I sewed the final version. I decided to leave this boo-boo so you could benefit from my mistake. It's really not that noticeable. If someone points out a blooper on your finished quilt, it's OK to pull out the "only God is perfect" card. This refers to the historical practice of sewing deliberate errors into a quilt so God wouldn't assume the quilt-maker was competing with his own patent on perfection.

TEMPLATE	PATCH	PROCESS	FABRIC
E	1	Cut 8	1
E	2	Cut 16	2
E + E	3 + 4	Make 8 L and 8 R	4 + 5
F + E + E	3 + 4 + 5	Make 8 L and 8 R	3 + 4 + 5

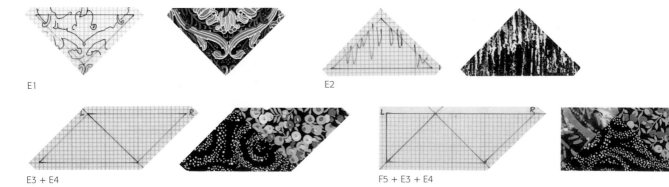

E1

E2

E3 + E4

F5 + E3 + E4

Fabrics 3, 4, and 5 are allovers and can be strip pieced consecutively.

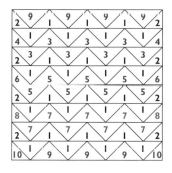

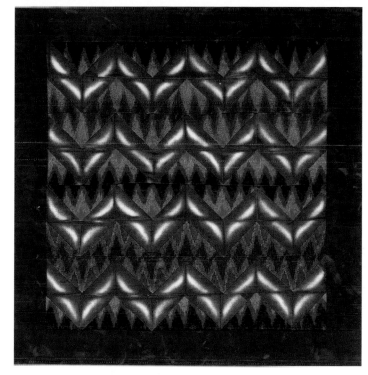

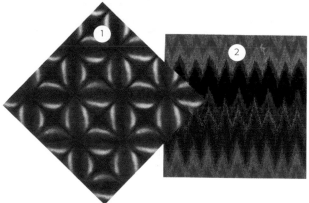

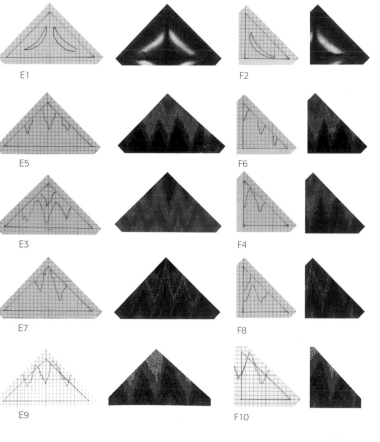

BLOCK 6D

These two fussy cuts merge successfully in an unexpected medley. The short white curves against black, like foaming whitecaps, compel the eye to run up and down the little hills on its journey across the block. The block reads differently, too, depending on whether the viewer is close up or far away. Up close, the differently colored rows of Guatemalan zigzags seem to have equal weight, whereas the impression from afar is of repeating red and white rows.

TEMPLATE	PATCH	PROCESS	FABRIC
E	1	Cut 28	1
F	2	Cut 4 L and 4 R	1
E	3	Cut 7	2
F	4	Cut 1 L and 1 R	2
E	5	Cut 7	2
F	6	Cut 2 L and 2 R	2
E	7	Cut 7	2
F	8	Cut 1 L and 1 R	2
E	9	Cut 7	2
F	10	Cut 1 L and 1 R	2

E1 F2

E5 F6

E3 F4

E7 F8

E9 F10

BLOCK 6E

What if you cut the full spectrum of a rainbow-filled fabric into a pyramid of triangles? Each triangular patch would comprise two bands of color. Starting at the red selvage, and with the darkest red representing A, the layout formula would be AB, BC, CD, DE, and so forth, so that in a column going down or going up, the color toward the point of one triangle would be the color in the upper half of the triangle below it. In case you have your magnifying glass out, please note: There weren't enough bands of color to use each one only once. The result is a soft transition.

E

F

TEMPLATE	PATCH	PROCESS	FABRIC
E	1	Cut 4	1
E	2	Cut 4	1
E	3	Cut 4	1
E	4	Cut 4	1
E	5	Cut 4	1
E	6	Cut 4	1
E	7	Cut 4	1
E	8	Cut 4	1
E	9	Cut 3	1
E	10	Cut 3	1
E	11	Cut 3	1
E	12	Cut 3	1
E	13	Cut 3	1
E	14	Cut 3	1
E	15	Cut 3	1
E	16	Cut 3	1
F	17	Cut 1 L and 1 R	1
F	18	Cut 1 L and 1 R	1
F	19	Cut 1 L and 1 R	1
F	20	Cut 1 L and 1 R	1
F	21	Cut 1 L and 1 R	1
F	22	Cut 1 L and 1 R	1
F	23	Cut 1 L and 1 R	1
F	24	Cut 1 L and 1 R	1

1

16

17

2

15

18

3

14

19

4

13

20

5

12

21

6

11

22

7

10

23

8

9

24

BLOCK 6F

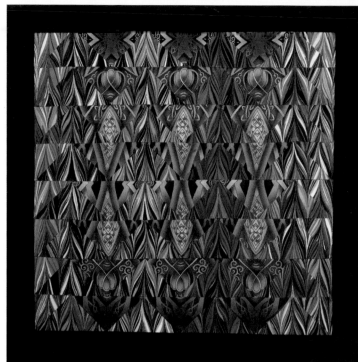

Here's a color strategy that keeps the values within a limited range. The seams between the closely related patches are barely discernible. The eye is vaguely aware of the identical motifs cut from Fabric 1 that peek rhythmically through the marbled textures. The image seems at the same time soft and blurry and rich and saturated.

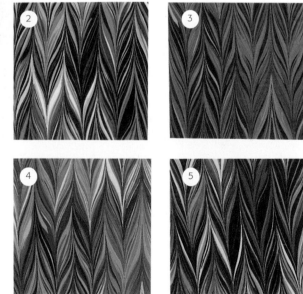

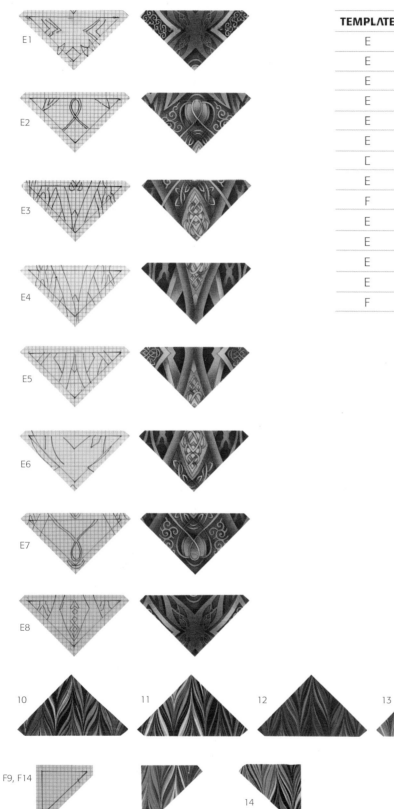

TEMPLATE	PATCH	PROCESS	FABRIC
E	1	Cut 3	1
E	2	Cut 3	1
E	3	Cut 3	1
E	4	Cut 3	1
E	5	Cut 3	1
E	6	Cut 3	1
E	7	Cut 3	1
E	8	Cut 3	1
F	9	Cut 8	4
E	10	Cut 8	5
E	11	Cut 8	2
E	12	Cut 8	3
E	13	Cut 8	4
F	14	Cut 8	2

BLOCK 1

Use Template A (page 92).

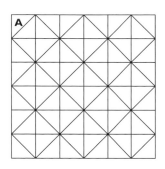 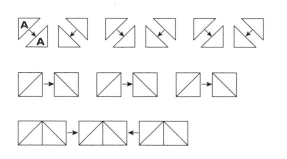 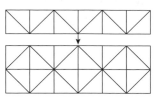

BLOCK 2

Use templates A and B (page 92).

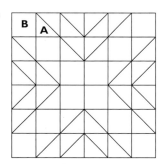 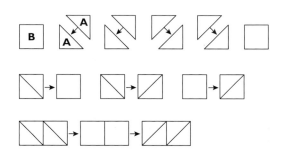 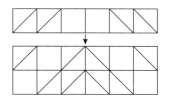

BLOCK 3

Use Template C (page 92).

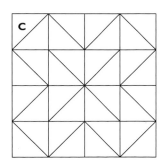 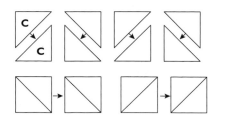 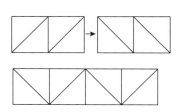

BLOCK 4

Use templates D, E, and F (page 92).

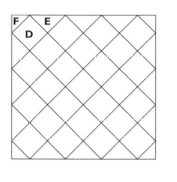
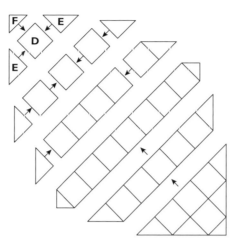

BLOCK 5

Use templates G, H, I, J, and K (pages 92 and 93).

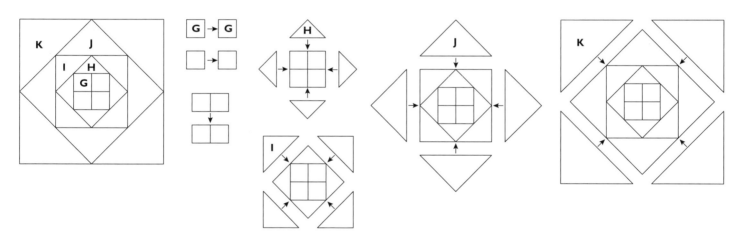

BLOCK 6

Use templates E and F (page 92).

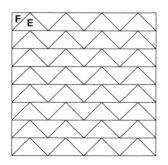
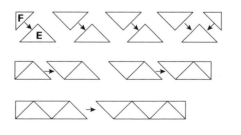
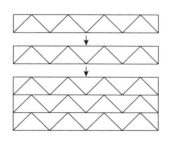

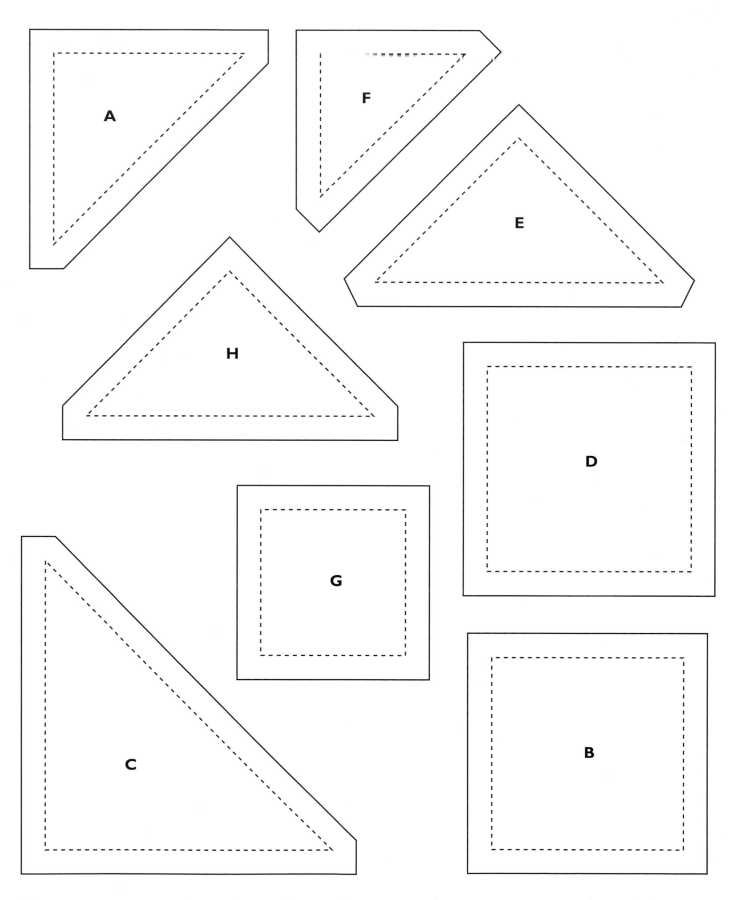

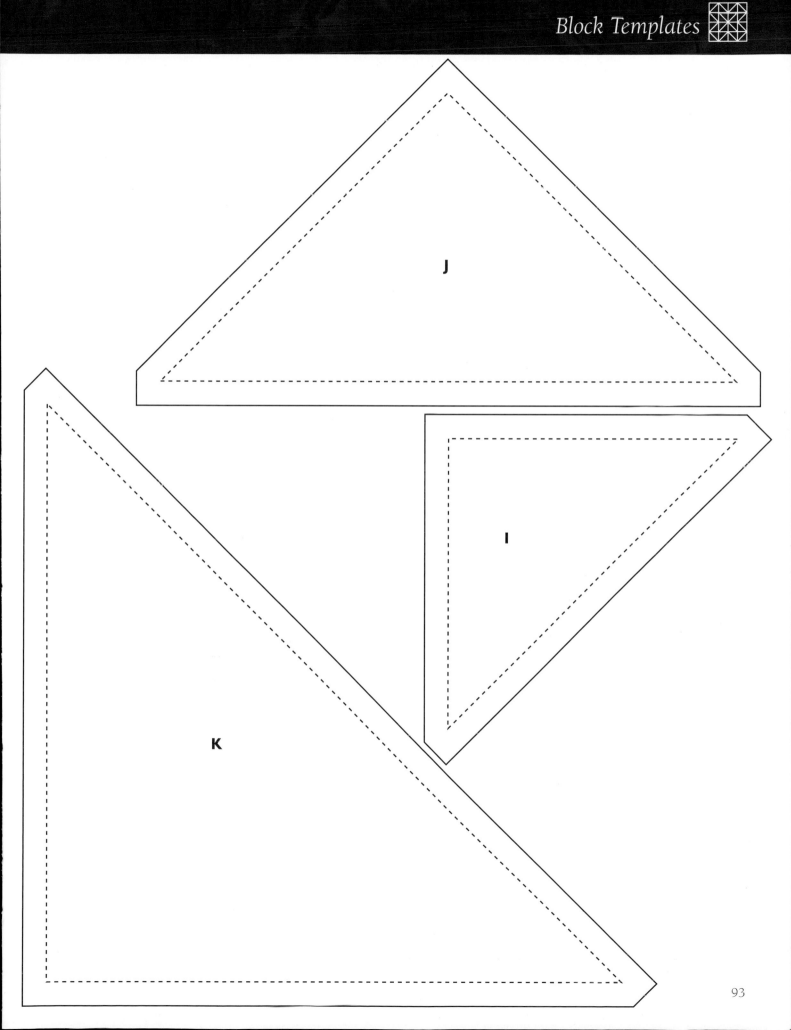

J

I

K

Use this page to rough out your own ideas in pencil or in color.

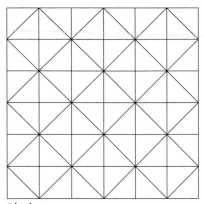

Block 1

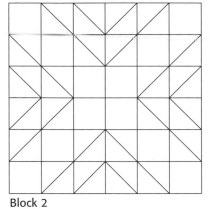

Block 2

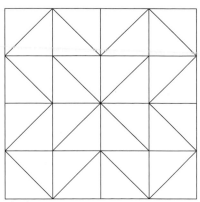

Block 3

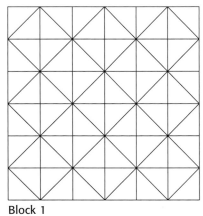

Block 1

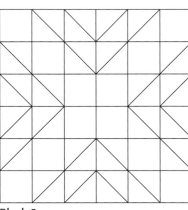

Block 2

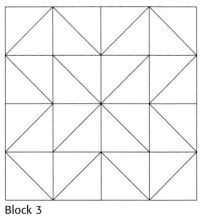

Block 3

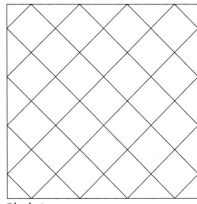

Block 4

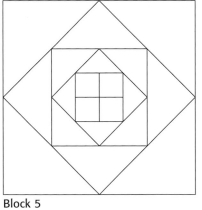

Block 5

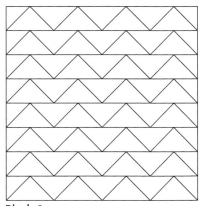

Block 6

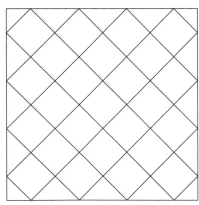

Block 4

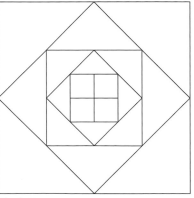

Block 5

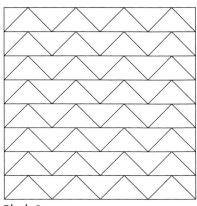

Block 6

Photo Credit: Bard Martin

About the Author

Paula Nadelstern's award-winning quilts have been exhibited internationally, in solo exhibits mounted at the Museum of the American Quilters Society, at the Houston International Quilt Festival, and in Japan, as well as featured in television shows, online websites, books, and magazines. Her work was included in the Twentieth Century's 100 Best American Quilts, a prestigious exhibit mounted for the millennium. Paula is the author of *Kaleidoscopes & Quilts* and *Snowflakes & Quilts*, and she travels extensively, teaching her unique kaleidoscopic quiltmaking techniques. She was a recipient of fellowships from the New York Foundation for the Arts in 1995 and 2001 and from the Bronx Council on the Arts in 1996. Paula designs textile prints exclusively for Benartex, Inc.

RESOURCES

BENARTEX
1359 Broadway
Suite 1100, Dept. PN
New York, NY 10018
www.benartex.com
Inquire about Luminosity fabric, designed by Paula Nadelstern, and Simple Symmetry and other simple patterns.

COME QUILT WITH ME
3903 Avenue I
Brooklyn, NY 11210
Phone or fax: (718) 377-3652
Source for the Brooklyn Revolver, a circular rotary cutting mat on a lazy Susan.

THE COTTON CLUB
P.O. Box 2263
Boise, ID 83701
Phone: (208) 345-5567
cotton@cottonclub.com
www.cottonclub.com
Source for Paula's fabric collections, prints with symmetrical motifs, see-through gridded template plastic, rulers and 8-to-the-inch graph paper pads.

COTTON PATCH MAIL ORDER
3404 Hall Lane
Dept. CTB
Lafayette, CA 94549
Toll free: (800) 835-4418
Phone: (925) 283-7883
quiltusa@yahoo.com
www.quiltusa.com
Mail order fabric and other sewing and quilting supplies.

DICK BLICK
Phone: (800) 447-8192
www.dickblick.com
Comprehensive art supply catalog; source for pens and graph paper pads.

DISPLAYAWAY
(888) ITS-SAFE (487-7233)
zellerwood@aol.com
Clever, safe, attractive display system allows quilts to be hung and removed in minutes.

GUIDE TO NYC GARMENT DISTRICT
www.paulanadelstern.com

INTERNATIONAL FABRIC
COLLECTION
3445 West Lake Road
Erie, PA 16505-3661
Phone: (800) 462-3891
Liberty of London tana lawn; fusible interfacing.

QUILTINGPRO
tgavin@quiltingpro.com
Management software for cataloging quilts and tracking shows and expenses.

STEINLAUF & STOLLER
239 West 39th Street
New York, NY 10018
Toll free: (877) 869-0321
Phone: (212) 869-0321
www.steinlaufandstoller.com
Notions distributor and source for feather-weight fusible interfacing (CL FW).